PRACTICING

THE PRESENCE

PRACTICING

THE PRESENCE

BY JOEL S. GOLDSMITH

Harper & Row, Publishers
New York, Hagerstown, San Francisco, London

CONTENTS

Except the Lord build the house, they
labour in vain that build it.
—Psalm 127

Illumination dissolves all material ties and binds men
together with the golden chains of spiritual understanding; it acknowledges only the leadership of the Christ;
it has no ritual or rule but the divine, impersonal universal Love; no other worship than the inner Flame
that is ever lit at the shrine of Spirit. This union is the
free state of spiritual brotherhood. The only restraint
is the discipline of Soul, therefore we know liberty
without license; we are a united universe without physical limits; a divine service to God without ceremony or
creed. The illumined walk without fear—by Grace.

—THE INFINITE WAY

INTRODUCTION

No one is going to pick up this book and read it unless it is someone who has already known quiet moments of inner reflection, someone who has been plagued by frustration, lack of success, or lack of harmony, and who has pondered long and seriously why life should be so unsatisfactory. Because this was my experience and because that experience led to the writing of this book, only those who have had a similar experience and have been goaded by that same unfathomable question will be interested in reading further to discover what I have found and how it has benefited me.

There have been many times in my life when I have had reason to be dissatisfied with the way life was going, dissatisfied to the point of quietly, inwardly wondering and pondering the possibility of finding a way out. Long periods of success and happiness, followed by dissatisfaction and unhappiness, finally led to longer and more frequent periods of introspection, cogitation, and contemplation of life, and what it was all about. In one of these experiences, while I cannot say that I heard a voice, I do know that I received an impression that was something like an inner being saying to me, "Thou wilt keep him in perfect peace whose mind is stayed on thee." I must admit that this was a startling ex- perience because up to this time I had been almost totally un-familiar with the Bible; it had not been a daily companion, but merely a matter of occasional reading.

Later, more thoughts of this same nature unfolded, and I began to realize that throughout Scripture we are told to "lean not unto thine own understanding. In all thy ways acknowledge him, and he shall direct thy paths. . . . He that dwelleth in the secret place of the most High shall abide under the shadow of the Almighty. . . . in quietness and in confidence shall be your strength." As passage after passage unfolded and revealed itself, I was led ultimately to that grandest experience of all, in which the great Master, Christ Jesus, reveals that if we abide in the Word and let the Word abide in us, we shall bear fruit richly, and that actually it is God's pleasure that we prosper and bear rich fruitage. Always there was the reminder that the price is: "Abide in Me; let Me abide in you. Abide in the Word, and let the Word abide in you. Dwell in God; live and move and have your being in God. Seek Him while He may be found."

Gradually, it dawned on me that all scripture was revealing to the world that "man, whose breath is in his nostrils," man separate and apart from God, is not to be accounted of, for he is nothing. I began to understand why Christ Jesus could say, "I can of mine own self do nothing"—of mine own self I am nothing; "the Father that dwelleth in me, he doeth the works." I could understand St. Paul when he said, "I can do all things through Christ which strengtheneth me," and then I knew what the missing factor was in my life. I had been and was living an ordinary, everyday life. All that God meant to me was an occasional reading of the Bible and an occasional attendance at church. Now I saw that the principle of life, the secret of all successful living, was making God a part of my very consciousness, something which Paul describes as praying without ceasing.

At first, you may not understand why praying without ceasing or thinking about God has anything to do with your being happy, successful, or healthy. You may not even be able to see what connection God has with the mundane affairs of life. This, of course, you are only going to discover through your own experience, because regardless of any testimony I may offer you of what it has done in my life, or in the lives of thousands to whom I have taught this way of life, you will not be convinced until you yourself have had the actual experience.

The reason you are reading this book is because you are being irresistibly drawn to God. There is a compulsion within you to find the missing factor in your life, that which will restore to you your original state of harmony, joy, and peace. Your having read the introduction thus far is an indication that this is what you are seeking, this is the need which clamors for fulfillment in you; and be assured of this, that from now on your mind will turn again and again to God, until one day, whether sooner or later, it will be made evident to you that your life will only be complete when it is lived in God and has God living in it. You will never feel entirely separate or apart from God, because never again in your life will you be able to go for long periods without bringing God into your conscious awareness and in some measure abiding in Him.

Think for one moment of what is taking place in the mind of the person who awakens in the morning and realizes, "Without God, I am nothing; but with God, all the powers of harmony unite in me to express themselves"; or who ponders some scriptural passage such as, "He performeth the thing that is appointed for me. . . . The Lord will perfect that which concerneth me. . . . Whither shall I go from thy spirit? or whither shall I flee from thy presence? If I ascend up into heaven, thou art there: if I make my bed in hell, behold, thou art there. . . . Yea, though I walk through the valley of the shadow of death, I will fear no evil: for thou art with me." Think of what it means to a businessman, leaving for his office, or to a mother, sending her children off to school, to know that they are not alone—wherever they are, the Spirit of God is with them, and where that Spirit of God is, there is liberty. Never again can they feel alone or that their life is dependent wholly on what they do or what others may do to them, for good or evil, for never again can they forget that there is a *He*, closer than breathing, nearer than hands or feet; there is a Presence which goes before them to make the crooked places straight, a Presence and a Power which goes to prepare a place for them. Never can they be separated from the Spirit of God as long as the Spirit of God is kept alive within them.

As you contemplate this, you will begin to discover that whether you are one of those who pray in holy mountains or in great temples in Jerusalem, or whether you do not pray in any particular place, the truth is that the place whereon you stand is holy ground as long as you are contemplating the presence and the power of God within you. That does not mean that you may not continue to worship in the church of your choice. This book is not meant to take you out of any church where, at the present time, you may be enjoying the association of those on your particular religious path, nor is it meant to put you into any church in which you may not already be worshiping. Its purpose is to reveal the kingdom of God—where it is and how to achieve it. The Master said that the kingdom of God is neither lo here! nor lo there! but is within you, and you will learn, through this study, that that kingdom is established in you

the very moment that you begin to contemplate His presence
and His power within you.

God *is*; of that you may be sure. This is only true in your
experience, however, in the degree in which you contemplate,
meditate, and keep your mind stayed on God, living, moving,
and having your being in the conscious realization that God
will never leave you nor forsake you. God's grace is your
sufficiency, but this is only made practical in your life by
your contemplation of that grace. Only in the degree that
you live consciously in the realization of God and let this
realization of God dwell in you does it become true that you
do not live alone—that the place whereon you stand is holy
ground, for God is with you and He will never leave you nor
forsake you.

Every person who has known dissatisfaction, incomplete-
ness, and frustration will some day learn that there is only
one missing link in his entire chain of harmonious living
That is the practice of the presence of God—consciously,
daily and hourly, abiding in some great spiritual truth of
scripture, and it makes no difference which scripture: Christian, Hebrew, Hindu, Buddhist, Taoist, or Moslem. The
Word of God, given to man through inspired saints, sages,
seers, or revelators—this is what we need, in any language,
from any country, just as long as it is a universal truth.

I have been a traveler for nearly fifty years, and I have
found peace, joy, and companionship wherever I have jour-
neyed. In my opinion, the reason I have enjoyed such satisfying experiences around the globe is because I have carried
with me the great truth given us by the Master, "Call no
man your father upon the earth: for one is your Father,
which is in heaven." This truth has been my passport and has
been the open sesame to freedom and joy in all countries, for
wherever I have traveled, I have consciously remembered
that God is the Father, the creative principle, the life of all
with whom I come in contact. No one can change the fact

that whatever the name, nationality, race, or creed, there is only one God, one Father, and that we are all children of that one Father; but this truth serves only those who consciously remember it, realize it, believe it, and trust it.

In my lifetime, I have known abundance and the absence of abundance, but in every case, whenever there has been a lack of any kind, harmony, wholeness, and completeness have been restored through the realization that "man shall not live by bread alone, but by every word that proceedeth out of the mouth of God. . . . I have meat to eat that ye know not of." Have you ever wondered what the Master meant by those words? Over the years, I have spent weeks and months pondering them, sometimes weeks at a time, and the next year more weeks, until I understood their meaning. I realized that he was talking about an inner substance, which made meat on the outer plane of comparative unimportance—not that he would not eat in due time, but when there were more important things to do, he had another kind of meat and bread to sustain him.

After the years that I have spent in this work, I can say to you that the inner meat, the inner water, the inner wine, and the bread of life—all these are brought into tangible experience through inner communion and in no other way. They cannot be brought from the outside into the inside. Not even reading the Bible will do this for you. It is taking the truths of the Bible into meditation and gaining an inner realization of them which changes the words that you read in a book into the Word of life, the bread of life, the meat, the wine, and the water of life.

Spiritual truth in a Bible is only a power in proportion as it is brought alive in your consciousness and kept alive. This is not my word to you; this is the word of the masters who have told us that we shall be kept in peace by keeping our mind stayed on God and that if we abide in the Word of God and let the Word abide in us we shall bear fruit richly.

We shall then have an inner water, an inner wine, an inner meat, and an inner bread to bring to the development and the growth of the fruit that is to appear in the without. You can only feed the tree of life from within, not from without.

The bread of life, the meat, the wine, the water—these are formed inside of us through the contemplation of God, the things of God, and the Word of God. These are formed within us by communion with the Spirit. Always remember: The Spirit of God is within you, but it is only the few today who seem capable of spending hours with spiritual literature, and more hours in inner communion—only the few. Their earnest desire to know God will insure their success on the spiritual path.

The message of this book is not a personal message. It is an age-old wisdom that man shall not live by bread alone but by every word remembered in consciousness, by every word and thought of God held within us. By this we live. When we try to live without God, we are living only with the carnal weapons of this world. When, however, we take this great truth into our consciousness and let it abide in us, then we are clad in spiritual armor, and the only sword we need is the sword of the Spirit. And what is the sword of the Spirit except every word that proceedeth out of the mouth of God?

I have learned, and so I endeavor to pass on to you: Keep the Word of God alive in your mind, in your thought, and in your experience, and you will never know lack or limitation. Keep consciously before you the truth that no man on earth is your father—there is only one Father, the creative Principle of all mankind—and you will never know anything but love from the men and women of this world.

As you keep the word of God alive in your consciousness, you are practicing the principles of spiritual living. In this book, you will find an exposition of these principles, which I refer to from time to time as the letter of truth. In and of itself, this is not sufficient "for the letter killeth, but the spirit giveth life."

This book is my personal life revealed. This book, *The Art of Meditation*,[1] and *Living The Infinite Way*[2] reveal all that has happened to me in my entire spiritual career, and not only to me but to all those who have been taught in this way, whether by me or by any other spiritual teacher on this particular path. For it is not I alone who have learned this secret of the Master; it is an ancient wisdom lived many times by many men. Throughout all centuries this way of life has been practiced, but it has been lost except to those few who live the mystical life.

The world's troubles in these past generations have driven men to seek that which will restore the lost years of the locusts, that which will establish peace on earth and good will to men. I have found it—and in this book, you will find it.

[1] By the author (New York: Harper & Brothers, 1956).
[2] By the author (London: George Allen and Unwin Ltd., 1956).

CHAPTER I

SPIRITUAL CONSCIOUSNESS

The secret of harmonious living is the development of spiritual consciousness. In that consciousness, fear and anxiety disappear, and life becomes meaningful with fulfillment as its keynote.

The degree of spiritual consciousness which we attain can be measured by the extent to which we relinquish our dependence on the external world of form and place our faith and confidence in something greater than ourselves, in the Infinite Invisible, which can surmount any and every obstacle. It is an awareness of the grace of God.

There is a specific practice which will aid in the attainment of this spiritual consciousness. It is a practice which can be carried on throughout the day as the world crowds in upon us, reminding us that we need this or desire that. To every such insistent demand, let our answer be: "No, no. This is not what I need or want. *Thy* grace is my sufficiency, nothing else—not money, not marbles, only *Thy* grace." Let us learn to hold to that resolutely. If the need seems to be railway fare, rent, clothing, housing, or health, let us steadfastly acknowledge that our only need is His grace.

Our work may require greater strength, greater knowledge, or greater ability than we seem to possess, or there may be greater demands made upon our purse than we can meet. Instead of accepting this apparent lack, let us remember, "He performeth the thing that is appointed for me. . . . The Lord will perfect that which concerneth me," or some other scriptural passage. The human belief may be that there is a physical, mental, moral, or financial demand made upon us greater than our ability to fulfill; but the very moment we turn to that *He* that is within us, recognizing that He performeth that which is given us to do, He perfecteth that which concerneth us, a weight drops off our shoulders, and the sense of personal responsibility lifts. All of a sudden, we are given the necessary ability, which we discover is not our ability at all; it is His ability being expressed through us. Out of our weakness comes strength, but not our strength; it is His strength, and we perform the work through His strength. If it is rest that we need, we turn to Scripture and find: "Come unto me, all ye that labour and are heavy laden, and I will give you rest."

One of the most comforting passages in Scripture is: "My peace I give unto you: not as the world giveth, give I unto you." If we could spend a month with that statement, it would open a whole new world to us. We might ask ourselves what we know about peace. We all know the kind of peace that the world can give, but that is not the kind of peace that we need. Many of us think we would have peace, if we had enough supply, or if we had our health, or if we had the right kind of companionship. That might be true, but having those things does not guarantee that we shall not be disturbed about something else. As long as we look to people and situations for peace, we shall fail to find either enduring satisfaction or peace: "My peace . . . not as the world giveth," but *"My peace."* "My peace" is a gentle spirit which wells up within us and has no relationship to the state of our affairs, although, ultimately, it settles all our affairs.

Faith in the Infinite Invisible deepens and increases, as we learn to depend consciously on the *He* that performeth that which is given us to do. That He, the Infinite Invisible, performs whatever is given us to do in the visible world. The Infinite Invisible perfects that which concerneth us. The Invisible Grace is our sufficiency in all things. The Invisible Presence goes before us to make the crooked places straight.

Gradually, as over and over again the temptation comes to say, "I need; I want; I haven't enough; I am insufficient"; we remember that our sufficiency is in the Infinite Invisible. This practice deepens spiritual consciousness. Brother Lawrence called it practicing the presence of God. The Hebrews called it keeping the mind stayed on God and acknowledging God in all ways. Jesus called it abiding in the Word. It is a practice that ultimately leads to a complete reliance on the Infinite Invisible, which in its turn brings the visible into our awareness as we have need of it.

Material living puts its faith in forms of good. Spiritual living makes use of that which is in the world; it enjoys the form, but its reliance is on that which is the substance of the form, or that which has created the form, the Invisible. All spiritual revelation has shown that the substance of this universe is in us. *Our consciousness is the substance of our world.* Therefore, in the Master's words, "Destroy this temple, and in three days I will raise it up." If anything in the world of effect is destroyed, in a short period of time it can be rebuilt, re-established.

Great civilizations have been destroyed, and others have taken their place. Anything that has been built can be rebuilt, because everything that exists in the outer realm exists as an activity of consciousness. If we should lose our home, our fortune, or our family, we can be certain that the consciousness that built it could rebuild it.

As consciousness becomes more spiritual, confidence in the Infinite Invisible increases, and our love, hate, or fear of the external diminishes. We see the Infinite Invisible as the law, cause, and activity of all that is and drop concern for the form, whether it be person, thing, or condition. The realization of the Invisible as the substance of all form is vital to the attaining of spiritual consciousness. The visible form is merely the natural result of the activity of the invisible law and cause.

Every issue of life is determined, not by external conditions and things, but by our consciousness. For example, the body, in and of itself, has no power, no intelligence, and is not responsible for its actions. A hand, left to itself, would remain right where it is, forever and forever. There must be something to move it, and that something we call "I." That "I" determines how this hand will be used; the hand cannot determine that in and of itself. The hand exists as an effect or as a form, and it responds to direction. As a vehicle or tool, it is obedient to us, and we impart to it whatever of usefulness it has. This idea can be applied to other parts of the body. The consciousness that formed the body in the beginning is the consciousness that maintains and sustains it. God gave us dominion through consciousness, and this consciousness, which is the creative principle of our body, must also be its sustaining and maintaining principle.

Once we catch this principle, we shall have caught the entire principle of life. Literally, the kingdom of God is within us; literally, the law of life—the substance, the activity, the intelligent direction of life—is within us. We have only to prove this in some one direction and we shall have proved it in every direction. If we can prove twelve times twelve apples to be one hundred forty-four, we can prove twelve times twelve to be one hundred forty-four, whether applied to apples or people or millions. If we can prove, in only one single way, that the kingdom of God is within us, and that the life, activity, substance, and harmony of our being are determined by the law of God within us, we shall have no difficulty in proving this in every phase of our life, in the health of our body, and in all the relationships of life.

The whole secret lies in the word "consciousness." An intellectual knowledge of the fact that God is all is of no value. The only value any truth has is in the degree of its realization. Truth realized is spiritual consciousness. If we are conscious of the presence of the Lord, if we are conscious of the activity of God, then so it is unto us.

God is love; God is life; God is Spirit; God is all. That is true whether we are saints or sinners; it is true whether we are young or old, Jew or Gentile, Oriental or Occidental, black, yellow, or white. There are no exceptions to God; God is no respecter of persons. There is no way in which God can be left out of Its own universe, but we can leave ourselves out of it.

God is; there is a God—never doubt that. This God is infinite in nature, eternal, universal, impersonal, impartial, and omnipresent. But how do we avail ourselves of that which God is? How do we bring this that we know about God into our individual experience? To illustrate, we can turn to the field of music. The principle of music is absolute. If, however, we fail to understand its principle and the sounds produced turn into a jumble of discordant noises, we do not rail against the principle. We apply ourselves more diligently to practicing the principle until we become proficient in its application. So it must be in our God-experience. God is, and God is here, and God is now, but God is available only in proportion to our realization and willingness to accept the discipline that is necessary for the attainment of that mind which was also in Christ Jesus.

It will do us no good to sit back and plead, "O God,

when are you going to act in my life?" Let us rather realize, "God is good. God's part is done. Thank you, God, that this principle is and has been available throughout all time. Now show me what I must do in order to avail myself of this principle, this love, this life, this immortal body." When we have reached that state of readiness, we have begun traveling the road which leads to spiritual consciousness.

Spiritual consciousness is attained through the activity of truth in consciousness. Dwelling on scriptural quotations or statements of truth helps to spiritualize thought. The more truth that we read and hear, the more active is truth in our consciousness. Thus we learn to abide in the Word. This is the first step on the Way.

The second, and more important step, is to be able to receive truth from within, to be receptive and responsive to the truth that wells up within us. Then we do not think, read, or hear truth with the mind: We are becoming aware of the impartation of the Word of God from within because the inner ear and the inner eye have been developed through our knowing the letter of truth and dwelling on it.

The letter of truth is made up of statements, quotations, and words, none of which, alone, is power. The only power is God Itself.[1] It is very much as if the shades on the windows were drawn, and we sat all afternoon talking about sunlight: what it is, what it will do, and how to avail ourselves of it. Then, after several hours, someone very skeptically remarked, "But, it's still dark here. After all this talking about light, it is still dark." Yes, it is still dark, and dark it will remain until we roll up the shades. So it is that we can talk about truth; we can read truth; we can study truth; we can hear about

---

[1] In the spiritual literature of the world, the varying concepts of God are indicated by the use of such words as "Father," "Mother," "Soul," "Spirit," "Principle," "Love," "Life." Therefore, in this book the author has used the pronouns "He" and "It," or "Himself" and "Itself," interchangeably in referring to God.

truth and never once feel the light, never once feel the presence and power of God, unless and until we take the final step of opening consciousness to the very presence of God. When truth comes to our conscious awareness from within our own being, we have gone from the letter to the Spirit. That is the most important phase of the activity of truth in consciousness.

The second step, which leads to a state of consciousness where we are receptive and responsive to the still small voice, cannot be taken, however, unless the first step has been mastered, that is, knowing the letter of truth. All the years that a person has spent in reading truth, hearing truth, thinking truth, attending church services, lectures, or classes are fruitful in leading him to that point where inspiration flows from within his own being. This inspiration, however, usually comes only after a thorough grounding in the letter of truth.

Jesus tells us to let "my words abide in you. . . . Herein is my Father glorified, that ye bear much fruit." To live in that truth, to abide in that Word, is to bear fruit richly, that is, to live harmonious, spiritual lives. But if we forget to live in the Word, to abide in it, and let it abide in us, we become as branches that are cut off and wither. How can we abide in this Word if we do not know it? We must know the truth. We must learn what the correct letter of truth is. Let us have a specific principle with which to work and let us stand on that principle, until the moment comes when we feel that spiritual awareness within us, which is realization. Then we shall know that we have attained the spirit of truth, the consciousness of truth, which is the Word of God and is power. Anyone with a sufficient desire for a realization of God can achieve that realization—the grace of God will guarantee it.

It is possible to know all the truth found in the letter of truth and still be a branch that withereth, until we so abide in the Word and let this Word abide in us that the very

Spirit of God dwells in us. There is a Spirit in man. There actually is a Spirit—the Spirit of God in man. No man is devoid of it, but most of us are as unaware of it as we are of the blood coursing through our bodies. God is with us. God's presence fills all space; the Spirit of God dwells in us. But how many people have felt that Presence? It is talked about, prayed about, theorized about, and sermonized about; but It is not experienced. It is the conscious awareness, the actual feeling or realization of the Presence which is necessary.

How do we know when the Spirit of God dwells in us? If we are letting go of hate, envy, jealousy, malice, self-seeking, self-glorification, prejudice, and bigotry, we are making room for the Spirit of God, for God cannot dwell in the midst of such qualities. As long as these qualities are present in our consciousness, we have more work to do abiding in the truth and letting the truth abide in us, until such time as the Christ has come so alive that such mortal thoughts no longer touch us. Then the Spirit of God dwells in us, "which is Christ in you, the hope of glory. . . . Behold I stand at the door, and knock: if any man hear my voice, and open the door, I will come in to him, and will sup with him, and he with me."

In most religious teachings, we are told that the Spirit of God is everywhere, but that is not true. If the Spirit of the Lord were everywhere, everybody would be free, healthy, wealthy, independent, joyous, and harmonious. No, the Spirit of the Lord is present only where it is realized. Unless we feel the actual presence of God, then, as far as we are concerned, we do not have this Spirit. Again, it is a case of rolling up the window shades, or it is like saying that electricity is everywhere. That is true. Electricity is everywhere, just as the Spirit of God is everywhere. Electricity, however, will be of no value to us, unless it is connected in some way for our particular use. So it is with this Spirit of God. It is everywhere, in an absolute, spiritual sense, but It is only effective in our experience to the extent to which It is realized.

The student of spiritual wisdom cannot go through his day, satisfied that he has read some truth in the morning, or that he is going to hear some truth in the afternoon or evening. There must be a conscious activity of truth going on all the time. That does not mean that we neglect our human duties and activities; it means that we train ourselves to have some area in consciousness always active in truth. Whether we look out at forms of nature such as trees, flowers, or oceans, or whether we are meeting people, we find some measure of God in each experience. We train ourselves to behold the presence and activity of God in everything around us and to abide in the Word.

The goal is very close to us, but nevertheless, as close as it seems, it is far away, because with every horizon reached, another beckons beyond. As we go forward in our quest or search, we can measure our progress in this way: We see the horizon before us and we have the feeling, "Oh, I have just a short distance to go." Sometimes, it takes only a few weeks or months to reach that horizon, and the whole world of Spirit is spread out before us. Then we believe we really have entered the kingdom of heaven, and we have—for a few days. Suddenly, we become accustomed to this light and we are aware of another horizon that urges us forward, another advance that must be traveled step by step, and again, we press forward.

It is important to learn all that we can about the correct letter of truth, to understand every principle, and then to practice these principles until we go from an intellectual knowledge to an inner awareness of them. We build our foundation on specific principles. Some of these principles are found in scripture: Christian, Hebrew, and Oriental. Some of them are not found in any written form, but nevertheless, they are known to all the mystics of the world. The further we go in this work, the more necessary it is that we know every one of these principles. They are the foundation of our understanding and they must become so much a part of us that when we are faced with a problem, we do not have to think consciously of any of them.

After many years spent in study and practice, mathematicians can give the answer to many a problem the moment it is stated; they do not require even paper and pencil for their calculations. An architect can draw a sketch of a beautiful home in such a short time that one marvels at his ability. An experienced lawyer becomes so familiar with statutes and court decisions that he either knows the law as it applies to a case or knows where to find it almost immediately; but if he were questioned as to his knowledge, he would probably say, "It has taken me twenty years to arrive at the place where I can do this."

So it is with us. Every time we are called upon for help, God puts the necessary words in our mouth. Sometimes there are no words at all, just a smile. To a person experiencing financial difficulty, it may mean, "Son, thou art ever with me, and all that I have is thine"; to one alone feeling the need for companionship, "I will never leave thee nor forsake thee"; to one struggling with a physical problem, "Thou art whole"; to one laboring under the weight of guilt, "Neither do I condemn thee. Go and sin no more."

If we solve enough problems and seek to understand the truth behind issues and situations, day in and day out for one, two, three, or more years, we shall have all the answers available for instant use. Years and years of contemplating God and the things of God, meditating and communing with God, will have eliminated the necessity for taking thought for the things of this world. When a question arises, the right answer is immediately revealed. The listening attitude, the expectant attitude, developed through meditation, creates a kind of vacuum into which God rushes with those things of which we have need, whether it be wisdom, power, grace, or whatever may be necessary.

An understanding of the principles of spiritual living, that is, a knowledge of the correct letter of truth, is necessary. That is the foundation upon which we build, so that we understand where we are going and why, and what our relationship to God and our fellowman is. It is necessary that we know these things so that we do not stumble into a blind faith that at some time or other may desert us. We need to know the correct letter of truth in order that we do not find ourselves in a state of mental chaos, relying on one thing today and on another tomorrow, never coming to an understanding of that which *is*. A spiritual life cannot be built without an understanding of God—the nature and character of God, the nature of God's law, and the nature of God's being.

Take scriptural passages which embody spiritual principles and live with them. Hold them up as a banner in the presence of any and every form of discord, until such time as these principles become automatic. This is dwelling in the secret place of the most High, living, moving, and having our being continuously in the consciousness of God, not just for a few minutes while reading a book or listening to a lecture. Despite the demands which are made upon us by the world, we must pause at frequent intervals during the day and during the night for the practice of the Presence. This need not interfere with our daily activities, nor does it mean that we must stop what we are doing. We can be standing right over the cook-stove or running a lawn mower and all the time keep our consciousness open to God, remembering that "My grace is sufficient for thee"; we can be out on the street, in the shops, or driving our car, always remembering:

The Spirit of the Lord God is upon me, and that Spirit is peace and joy to me and to all those who come within range of my consciousness.[2]

It is important that we let no hour of the day go by without some conscious reminder within us that the goal of life is to attain that mind which was also in Christ Jesus. The goal of the spiritual life is to attain God-consciousness—to live and move and have our being in an eternal awareness of God's presence.

Understand clearly that all spiritual wisdom is made up of two parts: first, knowing the truth, and secondly, having that mind in you which was also in Christ Jesus. Take certain of these specific principles which you will find stated in this book and live by them. Take them one by one. Carry one of them with you day in and day out for a week or a month. Then take another and live with it, using it as a yardstick with which to measure every experience.

It is possible for anyone to change the trend of his life, not by hearing or reading truth, but by making it an active part of his consciousness in daily experience, until it becomes a habit every moment of the day, instead of an occasional thought. Let these principles operate in consciousness morning, noon, and night, until gradually the actual awareness comes. Then we make the transition from being hearers of the Word to being doers of the Word. Then we shall be abiding in the Word and shall bear fruit richly.

[2] The italicized portions of this book are spontaneous meditations which have come to the author during periods of uplifted consciousness and are not in any sense intended to be used as affirmations, denials, or formulas. They have been inserted in this book from time to time to serve as examples of the free flowing of the Spirit. As the reader practices the Presence, he, too, in his exalted moments, will receive ever new and fresh inspiration as the outpouring of the Spirit.

CHAPTER II

DEMONSTRATE GOD

What are we seeking? Is it God that we are seeking, or are we seeking some thing from God? The very moment that we are looking for a home or companionship, the moment we are looking for supply or employment, the moment we are looking for healing, we are seeking amiss. Until we have God, we have nothing; but the very moment we have God, we have all there is in the world. There is no such thing as God *and.*

To seek for supply, health, or companionship is an impossibility spiritually, because spiritually, there are no such things. Spiritually, there is only God; but in attaining God, we attain all that God is, that is, God appearing as all form. Let us not seek the forms of God but seek the allness of God, and in seeking the allness of God, we shall have all the forms necessary to our own unfoldment.

Nothing is more important than this point: Are we seeking a realization of God, or are we trying to reach God in order to get something through God?

When we come to any spiritual study, nearly always in the beginning we are seeking some good for ourselves. It may be a healing—physical, mental, moral, financial—or it may be peace of mind; but whatever it is, as a rule, we are seeking it for ourselves. Very quickly, however, we discover that as the light of the Spirit touches us, it is of benefit not only to ourselves but also to the world. The person who is studying and practicing the presence of God soon has no problems, no needs, and no desires. Those things which are necessary for his health and supply have a way of taking care of themselves.

God is working out Its life as our life. God is individual life. God is working out Its life in what appears to be the form of our lives. God is working out Its life as our individual consciousness. God is working out Its plan in us and through us. In this knowledge we relax and become beholders. It is no longer our life: It is God's life unfolding individually. God appears on earth as individual you and me, and as we step aside, we begin to see God shining through. The harmonies that we experience are in the degree of our knowing that this is God's life. It is only your life or my life when we take hold of it and try to manipulate it or do something with it or try to make something of it. Rather should we become beholders of God fulfilling Itself on earth, God appearing individually on earth, God incarnate on earth. God actually is living on this earth as you and as me.

When we desire only a God-experience, heaven itself will open and pour itself out at our feet in the form of every kind of good. Let us be expectant of a Christ-experience, of a God-experience, expectant of some kind of a spiritual impulse felt within. That is the demonstration we are seeking. Getting rid of some disease and demonstrating employment or companionship have nothing to do with a spiritual teaching. In a spiritual teaching, our desire is purely that we may know God whom to know aright is life eternal. When we have eternal life, we have all, because eternal life includes health, harmony, wholeness, vitality, youth, and abundance.

It would be an impossibility to find ourselves in the presence of God and find anything of a harmonious nature missing in our experience, because "I am come that they might have life, and that they might have it more abundantly." How could we possibly have the presence of that *I*,[1] the presence of that God, and not have life and have it more abundantly? But to seek people, or places, or conditions would be to seek outside the realm of God. In that way lies trouble. Many have been destroyed by the very things they have devoted their lives to seeking, but no one has ever been destroyed by seeking and finding God. Seeking God leads to realization, to the actual experience of God. The Master well knew that in that experience we have all because he said: "Your Father knoweth that ye have need of these things. . . . for it is your Father's good pleasure to give you the kingdom."

To comprehend the full meaning of the Master's statement, we must understand the nature of God. Probably all of us have been taught from childhood that there is a God, but few of us know what God is. If we could put aside all books, including the Bible, and live with but one question in our mind, "What is God?" meditating day and night on that question, ultimately, God Itself would reveal the answer. We would have to do this, however, with a mind completely free of all concepts of God and begin as if we were completely alone with God. We would not accept anybody else's opinion, anybody else's experience, or anybody else's point of view: We would have *our own experience with God.* If we could do that, we should find that, sooner or later, God would reveal Itself to us in such unmistakable terms that never again would we have any doubts as to what God is or how to pray.

There have been and there are men who have known God face to face. We can be assured of the genuineness of their

[1] Wherever "I" appears in italics, the reference is to God.

knowledge by the fruitage of their teachings. John was such a one, and to John, the nature of God was love. We might take the word "love" and see if we can arrive at some understanding of what that word means and how it would operate even on our level of understanding. For example, if we were completely and exclusively controlled by love, what would our relationship to our child be and what would our conduct toward that child be? Would we find in that love any trace of a desire to wound or to cause him to suffer in any way? Would we find in our consciousness any desire to put him in prison as a punishment for his sins, or to imprison him in a diseased body or a diseased mind? Would we find within ourselves a single trace of a desire for punishment or revenge? No, in love there is correction and discipline, but there is no punishment; there is no withholding of any good.

As we dwell on this, we shall gain an entirely new concept of God and begin to comprehend the secret of spiritual living. As long as we are clinging to a God who can give us anything—even good—we have not arrived at an understanding of the true nature of God. God has nothing to give us. Everything that God is, we already are; all that God has, is already ours. We can come into the experience of this by relaxing from the fear of what we shall or shall not have tomorrow. If some night we could sit at a window, noting how dark it is and watching the movement of the stars and the moon, and if we could just stay at that window all night long until the morning light breaks, and then with the coming of full daylight when the moon and the stars are no more but in their place is the sun, we might ask ourselves what part we have played in all this. What did we have to do with it? If we could watch trees or flowers blooming, and when they are in full bloom, again ask ourselves what part we have played in this, whether we have earned it or deserved it or been worthy of it, we should soon find that God brought all these glories to us without any question as to our worthiness or unworthiness.

God is infinite intelligence, infinite wisdom, and infinite understanding. There is never a need for us to tell God anything or to ask anything of God, except perhaps for more light, more understanding, more vision. It is God's function to govern Its creation, to maintain it and sustain it, and all of this It does without any help from man. God does not need the aid of man; God does not need any suggestions or any advice from man. We are God-governed only in proportion as we understand this and entrust ourselves to God's care. Any attempt to tell God what our need is, indicates a distrust and a lack of understanding of the nature of God and acts as a barrier, keeping us from the very blessings that are rightfully ours as heirs of God, joint-heirs with Christ in God. To know Him aright is life eternal; to know Him incorrectly is to set up a sense of separation between ourselves and that which really is our life and the continuity and harmony of our being.

We must understand the nature of God as fulfillment. That precludes the possibility of thinking of God as that from which we are going to get something. God is fulfillment. God is fulfilling Itself, just as the sun, shining and pouring forth its warmth and light, is fulfilling itself as the sun. We do not pray to the sun to send out more light or to give more warmth. If we were going to utter any kind of a prayer in regard to the sun, our prayer would be an inner realization that *it is*—the sun is shining; the sun is warmth; the sun is light.

So it is with God. We should never think of God as that from which we expect to derive some good. We should never think of God as that which can bring peace on earth. There is no such God. The only God there is, is a God who is life eternal: God does not give us life eternal; God cannot withhold life eternal; God does not give us life today or tomorrow and then withhold life when we are one hundred twenty. God *is* life eternal, and our prayer is the realization of that truth. God is fulfillment. If we are not benefiting by the grace of God, that has nothing to do with God but with our having removed ourselves, at least in belief, from the grace of God. Spirit is in no way related to the human scene. A spiritual God cannot be brought down to a material concept of life. Let us lift ourselves above the material concept of life into God.

To seek God without a purpose is the ultimate of spiritual realization. To achieve that realization, we must come to that place in consciousness where our whole heart and soul yearn for God, and only for God, rather than for any good, any harmony, any healing, or any peace that may come to us. In that state of self-surrender we can say:

I seek nothing but Thee. I must know Thee whom to know aright is life eternal. Let me live and move and have my being in Thee, with Thee, and I can accept whatever else may come. What difference, then, will it make if I have a body or do not have a body, if I am healthy or unhealthy? "In Thy presence is fullness of life."

When consciousness rises to that place of devotion where God is God to us, only for the sake of God, that is when we have attained The Infinite Way of life.

In The Infinite Way, life knows no limitation whatsoever. There is no longer any concern as to whether we are rich or poor, sick or well. Our only object in life is to know Him aright, to come face to face with God, to be able to tabernacle consciously with God, to be able to commune with God. This is a joy greater than has ever been known by the man of earth, regardless of how many millions he may have acquired or of how many honors may have been bestowed upon him. None of these equals the joy, the peace, and the infinite and eternal harmony experienced by the person who knows God. Now, there is a complete disregard of the outward effects which are the result of the practice of the Presence. The whole heart and mind and soul are centered on realizing the Presence so that we may come to that point within ourselves where the Spirit of God is upon us, and we experience that inner joy which is the Presence. We feel that pulsing Spirit down to our very finger tips. Our whole being and our whole body are alive and alert with It.

Meeting God face to face is the end of the road. There is nothing more to be desired. When we come to this point, we know exactly what Paul meant when he said, "I live; yet not I, but Christ liveth in me." It is almost as if we were looking over our shoulder and watching the Christ work in us and through us and for us. It goes before us. If supply is needed, It provides it. If a home is needed, It provides it. If transportation is needed, It provides it. We never have to take thought for these things; all we have to do is to continue our life of contemplation, and then we shall find that in our business, profession, or artistic pursuits, we shall have greater discernment, ability, health, inspiration, joy, and remuneration. However, we shall not be praying to achieve these results: They will flow of their own accord just as the sun rises in the morning or the sun sets at night without any conscious effort on the part of anyone. All that is necessary is to wait—just wait long enough and the sun will come up tomorrow morning and go down again at night. We shall have had nothing to do with it except to contemplate it, behold it, watch it. We did not have to pray to God about it, and we did not have to know the truth about it.

So with us. We learn not to try mentally to manipulate our lives, hoping that by affirming some truth something good will be brought into our experience. Life becomes a complete joy, because just as we need have no concern for the movement of the sun, moon, or stars, so we need feel no burden of responsibility for our supply or our health. All these are a matter of God's grace. Our only responsibility is that the Spirit of God dwell in us. At one time or another, we must begin to make the transition from being man whose breath is in his nostrils, who cannot please God and who is not under the law of God, to being the child of God. From that point on we cannot fail: It is only a matter of devotion.

We cannot use God, but we can yield ourselves to God and let God use us. We can contemplate the things of God and meditate upon the spiritual, invisible, and unseen, until we actually feel that spirit and presence of God within us. Then let our prayer be:

Give me more wisdom; give me more light; teach me how to abide in Thy Word. Let me want Thee for Thy sake only. Let me never ask for a single thing for any person. Let me tabernacle and commune with Thee. Let my only purpose be to unite with Thee.

An occasional contact with God, like the proverbial grain of truth, will work wonders; but we cannot expect a complete and perfect spiritual existence simply because once in a while we remember to turn to God, or to devote a few hours to the study of spiritual books. It requires prayer without ceasing to make life a continuous experience of good. Then we find that God, who is the all-knowing mind, the divine omnipresence, the divine omnipotence and omniscience, always goes before us to provide those things necessary for our experience. That is the reason we never have to tell It what we need; we never have to tell It that we need money, a home, companionship, freedom, food, or clothing. We never have to tell God anything about our needs.

God is the infinite intelligence of the universe, that which formed it, and that which maintains and sustains it without any human advice. If God can do that for this great universe, let us trust our individual being and body to that same Presence and Power.

There is only one kind of a prayer which honors God:

Father within me, so much closer to me than breathing and nearer than hands and feet, You are the all-knowing intelligence of this universe, the intelligence which created it.

You are the divine love which has supplied this earth with vegetables and flowers, diamonds, uranium, oil, gold, silver, and platinum. You have filled the heavens with Your glory— the stars, sun, and moon—and the oceans with the rhythmic activity of the tides. I acknowledge Your presence in all things and as all things.

Even before I pray, Father, You know my needs. Even before I lift my eyes or thoughts to You, You not only know my needs, but it is Your good pleasure to give me the kingdom. I turn to You now, not to tell You my need, but to receive the fulfillment of my need. I come to You now, not seeking things, not seeking persons, but seeking Your grace, Your benediction, the gift of Yourself.

Let the peace that passeth understanding descend upon me—Your peace, an inner peace, an inner grace, an inner joy, and an inner harmony. Let the Holy Ghost enfold and envelop me. Let the Christ-Spirit fill my Soul, fill my mind, fill my being, and fill my body. In quietness and in confidence shall be my strength, because the Spirit of the Lord is upon me. It is a power of peace and grace to all who touch my consciousness.

Let us go to God for the joy of experiencing God and then see what God does.

We can begin this moment to take an important step forward—give up desire. We must give up desire for any and every form of good. From today on, there is only one desire permitted us, and that desire is to experience God.

We must demonstrate God—not persons, things, or conditions. This is really the cardinal principle of the whole Infinite Way. The Infinite Way teaches that we have the right to demonstrate the Spirit of God, the right to demonstrate the realization of God; but we do not have the right to demonstrate any person, place, or thing. We must be very certain that we are seeking only the realization of God's grace, that we are seeking only to be in the Spirit of the Lord. "Where the Spirit of the Lord is, there is liberty" from all limitation, all discord, and all inharmony. Our entire demonstration must be the realization of God, the demonstration of God, the consciousness of God's presence.

Realization *is* demonstration. It is the realization of the activity of God in consciousness that makes all spiritual good appear. It is the realization of God's grace as our sufficiency that makes the demonstration. The realization of any spiritual truth brings it into manifestation as effect. Merely to say, "He perfecteth that which concerneth me" will do nothing for us, but a realization of this truth instantly makes it effective in our experience. Realization *is* demonstration; but it must be a realization of the kingdom of God, realization of the activity of God, realization of the Spirit of God, realization of God as one power, realization of God as one substance, realization of God as the only cause, realization of God as the all-in-all. *Realization of God is demonstration.*

If we know the correct letter of truth, if we understand that God's will is love, that God's will is life eternal, if we know that God's will is that we experience His immortality, the infinity of His being, we shall not concern ourselves with telling God about our needs. All we would do is live in the constant attempt to realize God more and more, to have a deeper and deeper realization of God, of that God who is our very own being. The joy of communing with God is enough:

Father, all I want is my relationship with Thee, my conscious realization of the Christ—not for any reason, just for the joy of sitting here with the Christ. Christ liveth my life. The moment I have Christ, I have no life of my own to live; the responsibility is on His shoulders. From now on all I have to do is to follow where He leads, into green pastures, beside the still waters.

To make the contact with the Christ, for no other purpose than to experience It, is the highest form of demonstration there is on earth.

CHAPTER III

GOD THE ONLY POWER

Thus saith the Lord, the King of Israel, and his redeemer the Lord of hosts; I am the first, and I am the last; and beside me there is no God.   ISAIAH 44:6

And thou shalt love the Lord thy God with all thine heart, and with all thy soul, and with all thy might.   DEUTERONOMY 6:5

Throughout all time, scripture has revealed that God is the only power, but who has accepted this literally? Even in the Bible, there are accounts of people fighting, one against another. The teaching of most religionists of the world has been that there are two powers, the power of God and the power of the devil: The power of God is good and blesses; the power of the devil is evil and damns. Always there are these two powers; always God is battling the devil for control of man's soul; and always the question is: Who is going to win?

Today it is the same story. Accidents, disasters, and sickness are explained either on the basis of two powers, or by making God responsible for these evils. How can God be held responsible for any evil in the light of the message and mission of the Master, which was the healing of the sick, the raising of the dead, the feeding of the hungry, and the overcoming of every kind of disaster. The Master said, "I am not come to destroy, but to fulfill," so none of these things can possibly be the will of God. In the presence of God, there is no evil.

If God tolerates the sin, disease, and death that we are experiencing, what chance have we to survive or overcome them? If God is permitting these evils, or if God is a human parent teaching us a lesson, how can we rise above them and return to the Father's house? From the very beginning of our spiritual study, we have learned that God is the one power, the all-power, and not only the all-power, but the all-good power. Is it then possible for an all-good power to create, permit, tolerate, or send forth evil?

In The Infinite Way, we engage in what is called spiritual healing so we must have a principle which is exact. There must be no deviation from it, any more than there is a deviation from the principles of mathematics or music. The spiritual healing principle is that God is love, God is life, and in Him is no darkness at all. He is too pure to behold iniquity. But if we can be made to believe that God tolerates sickness, knows about it, permits it, or is trying to test or punish us with it, we have lost all possibility of ever producing a healing. There is no denying the fact that this world today consists almost entirely of sin, disease, death, lack, limitation, wars and rumors of wars. Does that mean that God permits them? Not any more than the principle of mathematics is responsible for our mistakes in arithmetic, or the principles of music for our mistakes in singing or in the playing of musical instruments.

According to Genesis, "God saw every thing that he had made, and, behold, it was very good." Therefore, if there is a devil, God made it, and even the devil must be good. It is the setting up of the devil as evil and God as good which separates us from physical, mental, moral, and financial harmony. There is no mystery to evil. The Master's teaching is very clear on this point:

> If a man abide not in me, he is cast forth as a branch, and is withered; and men gather them, and cast them into the fire, and they are burned.
> If ye abide in me, and my words abide in you, ye shall ask what ye will, and it shall be done unto you.   JOHN 15:6, 7

If we do not let this Word abide in us, we should not be surprised at anything that happens to us, but we have no right to blame God. If we are not showing forth the health, harmony, and wealth, which are our spiritual birthright, it is because we are not fulfilling the terms of the agreement.

The agreement is that if we dwell in the secret place of the most High, none of these evils will come nigh our dwelling place. That is the principle. Are we dwelling in the secret place of the most High? Are we? We meditate for five minutes in the morning and read a book for fifteen minutes later on in the day, and then we think that we are abiding in the Word and dwelling in the secret place of the most High. This is not sufficient. We must read and study, meditate and ponder, hour upon hour of every day until we are living continuously in the presence of the Lord beside whom there is none other. Let us accept in our mind a state of consciousness in which we agree that God is all power, God is infinite, and beside God there is no other power.

In the forty-third chapter of Isaiah we read:

> But now thus saith the Lord that created thee, O Jacob, and he that formed thee, O Israel, Fear not: for I have redeemed thee, I have called thee by thy name; thou art mine.

If from the time we were small children, we had been taught this one truth, "Fear not; for I have redeemed thee, I have called thee by thy name; thou art mine," would we ever have known fear?

When thou passest through the waters, I will be with thee; and through the rivers, they shall not overflow thee: when thou walkest through the fire, thou shalt not be burned; neither shall the flame kindle upon thee.

For I am the Lord thy God, the Holy One of Israel, thy Saviour. . . .

Since thou wast precious in my sight, thou hast been honourable, and I have loved thee.   ISAIAH 43:2-4

Can we not readily imagine the state of consciousness in which we would be living had we been taught exclusively and continuously throughout our childhood that God loved us and that He would not permit any evil to befall us? Then we would so live in the consciousness of God as the only power that we should never fear, nor should we ever lack for any good.

Yet now hear, O Jacob my servant; and Israel, whom I have chosen:

Thus saith the Lord that made thee, and formed thee from the womb, which will help thee; Fear not, O Jacob, my servant; and thou Jesurun, whom I have chosen.

For I will pour water upon him that is thirsty, and floods upon the dry ground; I will pour my spirit upon thy seed, and my blessings upon thine offspring.   ISAIAH 44:1-3

Throughout our youth, we were taught to look only to our parents, but here we learn that God "formed thee from the womb." We are children of God right from the womb, under God's protection, and God, and only God, has always supplied our needs and supported our activities. We learn that God alone is the only power in our lives from everlasting to everlasting. In this understanding, we can see what would have happened to the devil: There would never have been the fear of evil or the fear of punishment. We would have found a love of God instead of a fear of God, and we would never have believed that God could turn His back upon us.

To know God is to love God. As a matter of fact, it is only as we understand the nature of God that we are able to love the Lord our God with a love so great that not even husband, wife, or child will come before God in our heart and soul. God then becomes a living being, not to be feared but to be revered, to be loved, to be welcomed every moment of every day, and not just for an hour on Sunday. There is not a moment of the day that we cannot consciously keep God alive in our hearts by the remembrance that God *is:*

God is the intelligence of the universe, the love of the universe, the omnipresent Spirit that created, maintains, and sustains the universe. God is the source of the beauty of the trees and flowers and fruits. God is the very substance of the vegetables and minerals. God is the substance of the gold in the ground, of the silver, the diamonds, and of the pearls in the sea. God it is that fills the sea with fish. God it is that fills the air with birds.

God is in the midst of me. Where I am God is, and God's love is forever enfolding me. God is the source of my being. God is the source of my supply, the source of the very food on my table. God it is that gives me my life's work to do. God it is that gives me the strength to perform it. "He performeth the thing that is appointed for me. . . . The Lord will perfect that which concerneth me. . . . He that is within me is greater than he that is within the world," greater than any problem that is in the world.

There is only one power, and God is that power. There is no power in effect, and there is no power apart from God. God is the life of all being. This truth has been in existence throughout all time and has been known to all peoples. In the sacred Hindu poem, *The Bhagavad-Gita*, translated by Sir Edwin Arnold as the beautiful epic poem, *The Song Celestial*, we read:

> I say to thee weapons reach not the Life;
> Flame burns it not, waters cannot o'erwhelm,
> Nor dry winds wither it. Impenetrable,
> Unentered, unassailed, unharmed, untouched,
> Immortal, all-arriving, stable, sure,
> Invisible, ineffable, by word
> And thought uncompassed, ever all itself,
> Thus is the Soul declared!

Here again we see that there is one life, and God is that life; there is one power, and God is that power. A consciousness filled with the realization of God as the only power cannot fear anything in the realm of effect.

Most religious teachings have not given us the truth that God is omnipotent in earth as in heaven, but the day is here when every knee must bend to the truth that there is but one power. All metaphysical teachings have their origin in the revelation of God as one. But what has happened to that teaching? It has been lost in a modern devil, mortal mind. Followers of orthodox teachings fear the devil, and those who follow the newer, more modern teachings fear mortal mind. Wrong and ignorant interpretations of truth bind us to the belief in two powers, but the answer is always the same: *God is the only power*. Every one of us in some degree in our human experience has accepted two powers: God and a power apart from God, a power that sometimes rewards and sometimes punishes, a power that is sometimes available and at other times cannot reach us—and we are now paying the penalty for such acceptance.

We must rise to a higher dimension of life in which we see that there is no power in any effect; all power is in the cause which produces the effect:

For my thoughts are not your thoughts, neither are your ways my ways, saith the Lord.

For as the heavens are higher than the earth, so are my ways higher than your ways, and my thoughts than your thoughts.

ISAIAH 55:8, 9

If we are not spiritually alert, however, we can be made to accept any kind of false teaching or propaganda if it is thrust upon us frequently and forcibly enough. Through the mass hypnotism of the press and radio, we have all been victims of propaganda of one sort or another, but none of that could reach us if we but accepted the teaching that God, the Infinite Invisible, is the only power.

In our frantic, modern-day race for supremacy in armaments and material strength, it becomes necessary to stop and ask ourselves: Where does all this end? Are superiority and size all there is to power?

. . . for by strength shall no man prevail. . . .   I SAMUEL 2:9

Be not afraid nor dismayed by reason of this great multitude; for the battle is not yours, but God's.   II CHRONICLES 20:15

Be strong and courageous, be not afraid nor dismayed for the king of Assyria, nor for all the multitude that is with him: for there be more with us than with him:

With him is an arm of flesh; but with us is the Lord our God to help us, and to fight our battles.   II CHRONICLES 32:7, 8

Those who are materially minded have but the "arm of flesh." Those who recognize God as the only power live without fear, with no concern for external power, regardless of its size. Whether it is a high fever, dire poverty, or a hydrogen bomb, it is but the "arm of flesh"; whereas we have that which is invisible; we have that which cannot be touched, for "no weapon that is formed against thee shall prosper. . . ." Just as David went forth to meet Goliath, armed with faith in God, so can we meet any suggestion of inharmony by our recognition of one power.

In the material sense of life, the word "protection" carries with it the connotation of defense or armor, of a hiding place from an enemy, or of some means of withdrawal from danger. In the mental sciences, protection implies some thought or idea, or some form of prayer that would save us from injury or harm. The word "protection" suggests a destructive or harmful activity, presence, or power existing somewhere from which we must find safety.

The moment the idea of God as one begins to dawn in consciousness, we begin to understand that in all this world there is no power and there is no presence from which those who are dwelling in the secret place of the most High need protection. We shall see this as we dwell on the word "omnipresence" and realize that in this all-presence of good we are completely alone with divine harmony—a harmony which pervades and permeates consciousness, and is in itself the allness and the onlyness of good.

Let us ponder this idea and meditate upon it. The revelation and assurance come to us from within our own being that this is true: There is but One, and because of the nature of that One, there is no outside influence for either good or evil. There is no presence or power to which to pray for any good that does not already exist as omnipresence, right where we are. In our periods of communion we feel the infinity of God's presence. There is no other power; there is no other presence; there is no destructive or harmful influence in any person, place, or thing; there is no evil in any condition. God is one, and there cannot be an existence separate and apart from that One.

The Master has told us: "There is nothing from without a man, that entering into him can defile him: but the things that come out of him, those are they that defile the man." We have accepted the universal belief of a power, a presence, and an activity apart from God; we have accepted the belief that some one or some thing outside of our own being can be a power for evil in our experience, and the acceptance of this almost universal belief causes much of our discord and inharmony.

As we consciously bring ourselves back, day after day, to the actual awareness of God as one infinite being, God manifesting and expressing Itself as individual being, we understand more fully that all power flows out from us and through us, as a benediction and blessing to the world. *No power acts upon us from without our own being.* It must become clear to us that nothing outside of ourselves acts upon us for either good or evil. Just as we have learned that the stars, the creation of God in the heavens, cannot act upon us in accordance with astrological belief; so we have learned that conditions of weather, climate, infection, contagion, or accident cannot act injuriously upon those who have come into a measure of understanding of the nature of God and the nature of individual being. We are constantly being reminded that we should become more and more aware of the nature of God, the nature of prayer, and the nature of individual being, so that we will understand ourselves as the offspring of God, of whom it is truly said, "Son, thou art ever with me, and all that I have is thine."

We must think seriously on this subject of protection because each day we are faced with suggestions of impending or threatened danger. Always some person, some place, or some thing is being presented as a destructive force which we fear or from which we seek a God to save us. God's allness makes it utterly impossible for any destructive or evil influence to exist anywhere—in heaven, on earth, or in hell— so let us not make the mistake of thinking of God as some great power who is able to save us from a destructive person or influence if only we can reach Him. Let us not make the common mistake of thinking that practicing the presence of God is just another means of *using* God, or another method of praying to bring God's influence into our experience in order to overcome discord, evil, sin, and disease. Its purpose is to bring to individual consciousness the awareness of God as one, of God as infinite, individual being, of God as all-presence and all-power. The universal belief in two powers, good and evil, will continue to operate in our experience until we, individually—remember this, you and I, individually—reject the belief in two powers.

In this age, protective thought is the realization that God's allness precludes the possibility of any source of evil ever existing in the world or operating in individual experience. Our protective work, or our prayers for protection, must consist of the realization that nothing has existed, exists, or will exist anywhere, at any time, in our experience of the past, present, or future, that is of a destructive nature. Through study and meditation, eventually we shall come to that God-contact within us, wherein we receive the divine assurance, "Lo, I am with you always," the continuous assurance of the one Presence, one Power, one Being, one Life, one Law in which there are no evil powers or destructive forces. It is in this awareness of oneness that we find our peace.

Students should take this subject of protection into daily meditation for a month or two, not mentioning it to anyone. They should not discuss this, but keep it secret within themselves until they arrive at a place in consciousness where they feel that God is one. The secret of protection lies not in seeking God to save us from some danger, but rather in understanding that safety, security, and peace are dependent on our remembrance and realization of the truth of God as one.

The world is seeking peace, just as it is seeking safety and security, outside its own being; whereas, no peace, no safety, and no security will ever be found except in our individual realization of God as one—the only being, presence, and power. We cannot tell the world about this peace, safety, or security; but we can find it for ourselves and thereby let the world see by our experience that we have found a way higher than superstitious belief in some power of good that miraculously saves us from some power of evil. We cannot tell the world that there is no danger from outside sources, influences, or powers; but our realization of this truth can make the harmony and completeness and perfection of our lives so evident that others, one by one, will turn to seek that which we have found.

Out of the teachings of two powers come the philosophies that cause men to disagree among themselves. There is no way to resolve these differences because those people who believe in two powers are working from an erroneous premise, good and evil. Always good and evil are wrestling with each other—and what a struggle it is! But what happens when men relinquish the belief in two powers and rest in the consciousness of the Christ? Then it is that they begin to understand what the Master meant when he said, "Thou couldest have no power at all against me, except it were given thee from above."

The mystics of the world, whether Krishna of India, Lao-tse of China, Jesus of Nazareth, or John of Patmos, have given us the revelation that God is one. The Hebrew mystics also knew this truth when they taught, "Hear, O Israel, the Lord our God is one Lord." Throughout Scripture we find, over and over again, assurances of God's love for His children:

Fear not: for I have redeemed thee, I have called thee by thy name; thou art mine.

. . . .

Even every one that is called by my name: for I have created him for my glory, I have formed him; yea, I have made him.

. . . .

Ye are my witnesses, saith the Lord, and my servant whom I have chosen: that ye may know and believe me, and understand that I am he: before me there was no God formed, neither shall there be after me.

I, even I, am the Lord; and beside me there is no saviour.

I am the first, and I am the last; and beside me there is no God.

And who, as I, shall call, and shall declare it, and set it in order for me, since I appointed the ancient people? and the things that are coming, and shall come, let them shew unto them.

Fear ye not, neither be afraid: have not I told thee from that time, and have declared it? ye are even my witnesses. Is there a God beside me? yea, there is no God; I know not any.

ISAIAH 43:1, 7, 10, 11; 44:6-8

And so, again and again, it is revealed that God is one God; God is one power.

They that make a graven image are all of them vanity; and their delectable things shall not profit. . . . Who hath formed a God, or molten a graven image that is profitable for nothing?

ISAIAH 44:9, 10

Each of us has made an image of God: One looks at it and sees Buddha; another sees Jesus. Each has formed a concept of that which he thinks God is, and then he worships and prays to that concept, while all the time God is saying to us: "Only *I* am God, not your concept. Only *I*, the Invisible, am God—*I*, alone, am God." We must stop making graven images in our mind, stop picturing what God is like, and trust the unformed Invisible which penetrates and interpenetrates all being.

"The kingdom of God is within you. . . . the place whereon thou standest is holy ground"; and even if that place seems, at the moment, to be in hell or in the valley of the shadow of death, God is right there with us. We must cease this nonsensical belief in a God who punishes and rewards, a God who is present when we experience a healing and absent when we do not experience the healing we expect. God is never absent from us except in our belief that there are two powers, except in our fear of other powers which we have set up in our mind. We not only fear these powers—we sometimes fear God!

In reality, there is only one power: There is no power of evil; there is no power of sin; there is no power of disease; there is no power of lack or limitation. God made all that was made; anything that God did not make was not made. The world seems to be filled with the power of infection, of contagion, of hereditary disease, the power of lack and limitation, the power of evil in many forms. It is true that as long as we are dealing with the human world in a human way there will be two powers: the power of good and the power of evil. That is the human picture. Some people are sick more of the time than they are well. The majority of people in the world are poverty-stricken. As human beings, we shall always have laws of sin, laws of sickness, laws of lack and limitation. There will be two powers as long as there is a human consciousness in the world, because the human consciousness, itself, is a divided household, divided into two parts, good and evil. A state of existence which transcends this and where these opposites do not operate, but where only one power, one law, operates is brought about as an activity of consciousness. No one can do this for us, but we ourselves.

God must become an activity in our consciousness, or we shall struggle through life as human beings believing in two powers and experiencing good and evil. We begin with the theme that God is one. God *is* one: "Hear, O Israel, the Lord our God is one. . . . Thou shalt have no other gods before me," no other powers, no other laws but one.

God is the only law, a law which maintains and sustains the harmony and perfection of its own creation at all times. Looking at the growing trees, we marvel at a law which makes them bud and blossom every year. There is a law in operation bringing forth their fruitage. The sun, moon, and stars, and the ebbing and flowing of the tides bear witness to a divine law governing the universe.

These are laws and cannot be changed. Everything that is permanent is supported by law, but the discords and diseases of the world come and go: They are ever changing; they have no permanence; they have no law to support them. If disease were supported by law, this law of disease could not be violated, and no one could ever be healed or be free of disease. But disease is not permanent. It can be healed—sometimes physically, sometimes mentally, sometimes spiritually.

To accept God as one is to accept only one law and that law the law of God, the law of good, always active and always present in our experience. There is no law binding us to any evil condition:

Truth, omnipresent in my consciousness, is the law of elimination to every form of discord in my experience. Spiritual law governs my being, my body, my household, and my business. Spiritual law governs my consciousness. Spiritual law permeates, maintains, and sustains me.

Every day we are faced with the temptation of death. It makes no difference whether we are being told about the death of a friend, a relative, or some stranger in a far-off country. Every day the thought of death is consciously brought to our awareness. Even though it may not concern us directly, the theme of God as one should be brought to conscious remembrance:

God is one life—eternal, immortal, infinite, never beginning and never ending. There is only one God; therefore, there is only one life.

Many students of metaphysics, who no longer believe in the power of a personal devil, have created another power separate and apart from God, a power in the form of a superstitious fear of wrong thinking and a faith and reliance on right thinking. Let us give up any such ideas, now and for all time to come. Human thinking is not power; the human mind is not a power. Did not Jesus refute any such idea when he asked, "Which of you by taking thought can add one cubit unto his stature?" Let us put the mind in its proper place as an avenue of awareness and not a creative faculty.

The creative faculty is deep down in the Soul. With our mind we become aware of the deeper truths and laws of God; but it is the Soul, which is God, that is the creative principle of existence. It is the activity of the Soul that is power, and out of it flow gentleness, humility, and patience, all of which Paul spoke of as the things of God which "the natural man receiveth not . . . for they are foolishness unto him: neither can he know them, because they are spiritually discerned." The "natural man" is the reasoning faculty. The things of God are received by the Spirit of God, the consciousness of God, the Soul which is a deeper layer of life than the mind. We use the human mind as an avenue of awareness, but we recognize the Soul as the creative faculty.

To give power to anything external to consciousness is idolatry. It is to recognize a power apart from God. We must come to the inner conviction that power does not exist in form—any form, no matter how good the form may be. The form may come and the form may go, but the Spirit goes on forever, renewing and re-forming. As human beings brought up in the material sense of life, we hold ourselves in bondage to form, and thereby we commit idolatry. In other words, we bow down and worship or fear some kind of a form. Let us not love, hate, or fear that which exists in the external realm, because it is not power. Once we see that God is the only cause, we shall not fear some other cause. Once we understand God to be the only substance, we shall not fear an over-substance or an under-substance. Life is an activity of consciousness reflected by the body, but life is not in the body. Love, peace, health, wholeness, and perfection are all activities of consciousness. There lies all power.

We must not try to hold on to the forms of body. We are not body; the body is an instrument for our locomotion at this particular moment. It is an instrument for our activity, but we are not body. We are not fingers, or hands, or legs, or hearts, or brains. We are spiritual entity and we have a body given to us of God, eternal in the heavens. Instead of trying to hold on to this form of body, we hold on to the truth of our own identity, and the body is maintained harmoniously.

The Master promises that if we are willing to lose our life, we shall gain life eternal. If we will stop trying to grasp our life, as if we could hold on to it or lose it, and instead, realize that all life is God's grace, we shall find life to be eternal.

The teaching is: Never worship effect; never hate, fear, or love any effect. To worship form is to indulge in idolatry. The very moment that any form becomes a necessity in our experience, we are placing our dependence, our happiness, and our joy in that, instead of in the Infinite Invisible which is the cause of the form, and we are idolaters. We shall continue to love all the good things of life, but we should never love them to such an extent that we are unwilling to see the form disappear and a new one take its place. All human relationships, whether they are relationships with parents, husband, wife, or children, are given to us for our fulfillment in this phase of our existence. Let us understand them, love them, and treat them as such, but remember that our life is hid with Christ in God, not in some outer form.

From morning until night, we are faced with appearances which would make us believe that there is power in effect. That is why, in a world so abundantly supplied with all forms of good—diamonds, pearls, silver, oil, vegetables, fish, fruit—people are still praying for supply. They believe that all these forms of good are supply, whereas supply is within themselves. These things are effects of supply, but it is consciousness that is the source of supply. Supply is spiritual, an activity of consciousness. At first, we may agree with this only intellectually, but the day will come when it will be spiritually discerned, and then we shall see that the world of supply is within, although it appears visibly in the without.

We do not see, hear, taste, touch, or smell supply; but we see the *form* supply takes. We become aware of the form of the various substances which our supply takes; but to realize that supply is internal, an activity of consciousness, is to make our supply infinite, whether it be of words, money, or transportation. If we see that supply is the invisible Spirit of God in us, then the effect of supply will appear in form. As rapidly as we use the forms as which supply appears, the invisible supply will again become manifest, because it is infinite; it is always omnipresent, and the supply itself, which is the Spirit of God in us, will reproduce it. No longer shall we live by bread alone, but by a consciousness of God's presence which requires no words, but rests in God as one.

As we persist in this throughout the day, the night, the week, the month, gradually we reach a point where the recognition of this truth is as automatic as driving an automobile. When we were learning to drive an automobile, we had to watch our left foot, our right foot, our left hand, and our right hand; but by the end of a month, we were driving without ever thinking of our hands or feet. So it is with this, at the end of a month, we shall find that we do not have to think consciously about God as one or God as life. We do not have to think of that at all, because it will be so much a part of our consciousness that the moment a suggestion of evil touches us, it is erased without any conscious effort on our part.

Now we have accepted as our principle: God is one; God is the only law; God is the only presence; God is the only substance; God is the only power, and there is no power in effect. Then in the next breath, we turn around and give power to some effect. What difference does it make what the appearance is, if God is the only power? *Do we really believe that God is the only power?*

God alone is power. God is one: one power, one life, one love, one Spirit, one cause, one being, one source. Nothing comes into our experience unless it comes from God. The next time something that we call evil comes into our experience, let us remember our principle and turn and say: "That, too, is from God. '. . . if I make my bed in hell, behold, thou art there.'" Even when we go down into hell, we find God, and in finding God, hell is transformed into heaven. A change takes place in our experience the moment we acknowledge no source, no cause, no effect, no power, no presence, and no being but God.

To practice this principle—hour after hour, day in and day out, for one month or two months, holding to God as the law of our being, God as the source of our good, God as the activity of our day—changes our entire experience. At first, this is all in the realm of the mind, but by constant practice, it leaves the realm of the mind and comes down into the heart, into the awareness, into consciousness. and then it takes over and lives our experience.

And thou shalt love the Lord thy God with all thine heart, and with all thy soul, and with all thy might.   DEUTERONOMY 6:5

CHAPTER IV

THE INFINITE NATURE OF
INDIVIDUAL BEING

T here is an old, old story about a great spiritual teacher who knocked at the gates of heaven for admission into paradise. After some time, God came to the door and inquired, "Who is there? Who knocks?"

To this query, came the confident response, "It is I."

"Sorry, very sorry. There is no room in heaven. Go away. You will have to come back some other time." The good man, surprised at the rebuff, went away puzzled. After several years, spent in meditating and pondering over this strange reception, he returned and knocked again at the gate. He was met with the same question and gave a similar response. Once again he was told that there was no room in heaven; it was completely filled at that time.

In the years that passed, the teacher went deeper and deeper within himself, meditating and pondering. After a long period of time had elapsed, he knocked at the gates of heaven for the third time. Again God asked, "Who is there?"

This time his answer was, "Thou art."

And the gates opened wide as God said, "Come in. There never was room for *Me* and thee."

There is not God *and* you or I, there is only God expressed, manifested as individual being. There is only one life—the Father's. We are outside of heaven with no hope of ever gaining entrance to it as long as we believe that we have a selfhood apart from God, a being separate and independent of God.

All through the ages, duality has separated us from our good, but it is a sense of duality, not duality, because there is no duality. The secret of life is oneness, and oneness is not something that we bring about. Oneness is a state of being.

Let us take, as an example, a glass tumbler and think of the outside of it and the inside of it. Where does the outside end, and where does the inside begin? As a matter of fact, is there an outside to this tumbler and is there an inside to it? Are there two sides to this tumbler or is there simply a tumbler? Is the outside not the inside, and is not the inside the outside? Are not the outside and the inside of this tumbler one and the same piece of glass? Does not the outside of the tumbler perform one function and the inside another?

When it becomes clear to us that the outside and the inside of this tumbler are one and the same piece of glass, we can then see the relationship between God and man. There is no such thing as God *and* man, any more than there is an outside and an inside to the tumbler, separate and apart from each other. The outside and the inside are one.

God is our invisible Selfhood: We are the externalized form or expression of that God, but we are no more two than are the sides of the tumbler. We are only two in function:

God is the creative principle, the source, the activity, and the law of our being; and our being is God in expression or manifestation. We, as individuals, receive our life, law, cause, substance, reality, and continuity from the Infinite Invisible, and that invisible activity appears visibly as the harmony of our being. To return to the example of the tumbler, we observe that any quality, which seems to belong to it, belongs to the glass of which it is formed. The glass then is the substance of the tumbler, and it is the glass that determines the quality and the nature of the tumbler. So with us. God, our inner selfhood, is the quality, the quantity, the cause, the reality, and the substance of our being. All that God is, we are; all that this inner selfhood is, is that which is manifest as my individual being and as yours.

God is no respecter of persons. God has no favorites— no favorite religion, race, or nationality. So far as God is concerned, God is one. The degree of our demonstration is the degree of our awareness of this relationship. If a person believes that he has a quality, nature, or characteristic of his own, he has set up a sense of limitation which separates him from the infinity of his demonstration. When he sets aside the belief that he has qualities, activities, or characteristics of his own and realizes that it is God, Itself, his inner Selfhood, that is appearing outwardly, and that it is this inner Selfhood that has and possesses all the qualities, activities, and characteristics of his being; in that moment, he has begun to die daily.

This is the meaning of Paul's statement, "I die daily." We must die to every suggestion that we are or have something of ourselves separate and apart from God. We must die to the belief of health just as we must die to the belief of disease. Spiritually, there is no disease, and there is no health because we are or have nothing of our own. To suffer from disease or to enjoy good health is to have something of our own. God has neither health nor disease; God is Spirit, and all that we can possibly have is the Spirit of God. We rise above this pair of opposites, health and disease, as we realize that there is no selfhood apart from God. The only thing that we can possess is what God possesses. God's selfhood is the only Selfhood—neither rich nor poor, neither sick nor well, neither young nor old, and neither live nor dead. It is a state of immortality, eternal being, unchanging, but nevertheless, infinite in its forms and appearances. To acknowledge no selfhood apart from God is the meaning of the Master's command to deny oneself. We should deny that we, of ourselves, have any qualities, character, strength, health, wealth, wisdom, glory, or potentialities. It is our inner Selfhood, God, which appears outwardly as you or as me.

The nature of our existence is immortality, eternality, infinity. Only by virtue of the fact that God is our being can anyone say:

I am infinite; I am eternal; I am immortal—not in and of myself, separate and apart from God, but because God is the life and substance of my being. Infinity is the quantity, and perfection, the quality of being.

The Word is made flesh; all flesh is formed of the Word of God. My body, therefore, is the perfect Word of God made flesh, made manifest. My body, being of the essence and substance of God, God-governed, can embody only the activity, harmony, grace, joy, and beauty of God. Nothing external can affect the perfection of my body, whether it is in the form of food, germs, or other people's thoughts. Nothing foreign to God can enter to defile it or make a lie.

There is a common belief that food has power to nourish us for good, to make us ill, or to make us fat or lean; but the fact is, our consciousness governs the organs and functions of the body. It is our consciousness, God-consciousness, which is our individual consciousness, that is the law, the cause, the activity, and the substance of the organs and functions of the body. That same consciousness is the substance and nourishment of the food we eat. The food, in and of itself, has no quality or property of nourishment except what we give it. Once we can agree that, in and of themselves, our digestive and eliminative organs have no power to act, but that consciousness is the animating power, directing their functioning, we can go forward to the next step and realize that it is this same consciousness which imparts to our food its value.

From the moment that we were conceived as human beings, we have been under material and mental laws; we have been governed by laws of food, weather, climate, time, and space. Always as human beings, we are under some law, whether it is a natural law or a law of materia medica or theology. These are really universal beliefs, but they act as law to our experience until we consciously realize our immunity from anything and anybody external to ourselves and realize that the issues of life flow out from us. We are not the victims of anything external to ourselves. We are spiritual identity, not mortal beings conceived in sin and brought forth in iniquity. Our true identity is consciousness, Spirit, Soul; and therefore, we are not subject to the laws of matter. God is infinite law, and this being true, the only law is the law of God, operating in our consciousness as a law of harmony unto our bodies.

If this realization were of great enough depth, we would automatically rule out of our lives all physical discords; but because in most cases it is merely an intellectual acceptance, it is not effective in our experience. Let us make it effective by a specific act of consciousness:

Spirit is my true identity. I have now come out and become separate; I am no longer of the world, even though in it, and therefore, I am not subject to the world's laws. None of these human beliefs is binding upon the child of God, the off-spring of Spirit, which I am. God is the source of my being; God is the activity and the law of my being, and I consciously accept that. I am not subject to man-made laws; I am subject only to grace. Thy grace is sufficient for me.

Let us take every detail of our life—our body, our food, our business, our home—and consciously make this transition: Realize that all these are no longer under the law of human belief, no longer subject to circumstance or change. All that concerns us is supplied from this infinite storehouse within our own being:

"I have meat to eat that ye know not of. . . . I am the bread of life: he that cometh to me shall never hunger; and he that believeth on me shall never thirst." From this infinite storehouse, I feed my body; I manage my business; I supply my pocketbook; I maintain my relationship with everyone. Since God is my individual consciousness, It is the substance of my life and It embodies all good. It becomes the law unto my experience, a well-spring of life gushing forth into life eternal.

God fulfills Itself as our individual being. If we can lose concern for ourselves, for our welfare, and for our destiny, God takes over and God fulfills Itself by providing us with the necessary wisdom, activity, opportunity, and prosperity that It may be fulfilled on earth as It is in heaven. This earth is only the earth in proportion as we see it as a place other than heaven. Earth becomes heaven to the degree in which we let God fulfill Itself as our individual experience.

There is only one Selfhood, and that one is God. We entertain a false sense of that Self: We call that false sense Bill, Mary, or Henry, and then we are concerned about Bill, Mary, or Henry. Always there is some problem to plague us: It is the rent; it is the heart; it is the mind; or it is the friend. This will be true as long as there is concern for ourselves. Once we give up concern for this human sense of self and realize that we exist as God fulfilling Itself in an individual way, and that the responsibility is on His shoulder, we relinquish this false sense of responsibility. Then God fulfills Its destiny as individual being. To the world, it may appear that we are healthy, happy, successful, or prosperous; but we know better. Only God is healthy, happy, successful, or prosperous, and the good the world beholds is God fulfilling Itself as our destiny, when we stand aside and permit it to do so.

In this God-relationship, we can relax because now all that God is, is permitted to flow into being without the word "I" interfering, the "I" that says: "I am not well enough educated; I am not sufficiently experienced; I am too young for this; I am too old for that." If there were only God, would there be any lack of education or experience, or any problem of age or youth? To God all things are possible.

God is the universal mind or intelligence, but God is also individual mind or intelligence. Therefore, the nature of our intelligence and capacity is infinity itself. Our mind is unlimited as long as we realize God as its nature, character, quality, and quantity.

We are told to have that mind in us which was also in Christ Jesus. We already have it, but it is necessary to attain a realization of it. It is this mind that transcends our education and experience and uses us for its own purpose, when we come into a conscious realization of it as our individual mind. The attainment of even a degree of this realization sets a person apart. It may lift him out of the ordinary, everyday pursuits of life and make of him a painter, artist, sculptor, musician, poet, religious seer, architect, builder, or a creative worker in one way or another because he is drawing on something greater than himself, something greater than his education or his own experience. Moses, a shepherd of the hills, became the leader of the Hebrew people. Jesus, whom neighbors knew as a carpenter, became the Messiah.

God is infinite consciousness, and God is our mind and our consciousness. Therefore, it is from your consciousness and from mine that the issues of life must come—the activity of supply, the activity of health, harmony, and wholeness. There is no far-off God to bring it to us. The activity of truth in our consciousness appears as the miracle of the cloud by day, the pillar of fire by night, manna falling from the sky, the Red Sea opening, water coming from the rock. God in the midst of us, this *I* at the center of our being, multiplies loaves and fishes, is our safety and security, even in the midst of war, even in the midst of atomic bombs, even in the midst of hell.

I am the Lord, and there is none else. I in the midst of thee am mighty. I in the midst of Moses made the cloud by day and the pillar of fire by night. I in the midst of Jesus multiplied the loaves and the fishes and healed the multitudes.

I AM is the Lord; *I* AM is the Saviour; *I* AM is God. This *I* is not the personal sense of selfhood which walks the earth calling itself Bill, Mary, or Henry, and saying arrogantly, "I am God." No, it comes as a gentle whisper in your ear and mine: "Know ye not: *I* in thee and thou in Me, we are one; *I* in the midst of thee am mighty." When we hear that spoken in our ear, when divine intuition within tells us of this Presence, we know that that *I* is God, "closer . . . than breathing, and nearer than hands or feet."

This *I* which is God has made us in Its own image and likeness, has given us Its nature and Its character. It is a Presence that will never leave us nor forsake us. Even if we go through the fiery furnace, this Presence, the Christ, will bring us safely through, so that there will not even be the smell of smoke upon us. Whatever the experience is in life, even "in the valley of the shadow of death . . . Thou art with me." We find our good in our oneness with God, and our consciousness of the presence of God appears outwardly as our daily supply, as our opportunity, as our clothing, transportation, food, and as every expression of harmony and beauty in life.

All the discords and inharmonies of the world come from the personal sense of "I"—from the sense that "I" am the source, or "I" am the doer, or "I" am something or other. But "I" am nothing of myself; the Father is that which I am, and "I" am but the instrument for the Father, the instrument of the Father's glory, the instrument of the Father's life, the lamp through which His light may shine.

"Rejoice, because your names are written in heaven." Rejoice that you have found your identity as a child of God. Rejoice that you have awakened into your heavenly consciousness. If the Spirit takes hold of your hand and begins to write, if the Spirit takes hold of your voice and makes it sing, follow the lead of the Spirit. Until that time, live your normal, natural life, but from morning until night, and night until morning, remember to acknowledge that it is the Infinite Invisible that is producing the harmony, the joy, the peace, and the prosperity of the visible experience. As you persist in this practice, you will make a conscious transition to a place where you will actually feel and know:

I am not living by food alone; I am not living by bread alone. There is another power acting in me. Something other than I is doing the work; I did not consciously plan it; I am not consciously doing it; I did not consciously think of it. A power greater than I is responsible for this.

"*I have meat to eat that ye know not of. . . .*" *I have*

bread, wine, water. . . . I am the resurrection. All the power of healing, redemption, and regeneration is within me.

This is the Master's transcendental teaching.

As human beings, we place our reliance on persons and things in the outer world, on education, money, bonds, or investments. That man who has his being in Christ places his entire reliance on Spirit and trusts it to bring forth all that is necessary in the outer realm. Whenever faced with some need or desire, let us realize Spirit as the source of its fulfillment; let us realize Spirit as the law unto it, even the law of multiplication should that be necessary. Then let us go about our business, whatever it may be, taking such human footsteps as may be necessary at the moment. This is living a normal, natural life, but letting the Spirit, the Infinite Invisible, be the law of it, the substance of it, the cause of it, and the harmonious maintainer and sustainer of it. In short, we make no change in our present mode of living, except as the Spirit, Itself, may pick us up and direct us into new activity.

There is a power governing us, caring for us, protecting us, maintaining and sustaining us. We may continue to be active in the business world, in politics, or in the home; but always present is that sustaining influence which goes before us to make the crooked places straight. The sense of personal responsibility and the fear of what man can do to us drop away:

I in the midst of me is mighty; I go before me to make the crooked places straight; I am with me in the deep waters; I am beside me in the fiery furnace.

It is the conscious remembrance of the *I*, the infinite nature of individual being, which must be continuously practiced.

Fulfillment comes about only as you and I are able to relinquish the personal sense of self, in order that God may fulfill Itself. Let us be ever alert to avoid any egotistical sense that God is fulfilling you or fulfilling me, is doing something for you or for me, or is doing something to you or to me. Spiritual fulfillment means God fulfilling Itself, fulfilling Its destiny. Let God be the only presence; let God be the only power; let God be the light. "Arise, shine; for thy light is come, and the glory of the Lord is risen upon thee." God's glory shines eternally as infinite, individual being.

CHAPTER V

LOVE THY NEIGHBOR

Thou shalt love the Lord thy God with all thy heart, and with all thy soul, and with all thy mind.

This is the first and great commandment.

And the second is like unto it, Thou shalt love thy neighbour as thyself.   MATTHEW 22:37–39

The two great commandments of the Master form the basis of our work. In the first and great commandment, we are taught that there is no power apart from God. Our realization must always be that the Father within us, the Infinite Invisible, is our life, our Soul, our supply, our fortress, and our high tower. Next in importance is the commandment to "love thy neighbor as thyself," and its corollary that we should do unto others as we would have others do unto us.

What is love in the spiritual sense? What is the love which is God? As we remember how God was with Abraham, with Moses in the wilderness, with Jesus, John, and

Paul, ministering to them, the word "love" takes on a new meaning. We see that this love is not something far-off, nor is it anything that can come to us. It is already a part of our being, already established within us; and more than that, it is universal and impersonal. As this universal and impersonal love flows out from us, we begin to love our neighbor, because it is impossible to feel this love for God within us and not love our fellow man.

> If a man say, I love God, and hateth his brother, he is a liar: for he that loveth not his brother whom he hath seen, how can he love God whom he hath not seen?   I JOHN 4:20

God and man are one, and there is no way to love God without some of that love flowing out to our neighbor.

Let us understand that anything of which we can become aware is a neighbor, whether it appears as a person, place, or thing. Every idea in consciousness is a neighbor. We can love that neighbor as we see him or it possessing no power except that which comes from God. When we see God as the cause and our neighbor as that which is in and of God, then we are loving our neighbor, whether that neighbor appears as a friend, relative, enemy, animal, flower, or stone. In such loving, which understands all neighbors to be of God, derived of God-substance, we find that every idea in consciousness takes its rightful place. Those neighbors who are a part of our experience find their way to us, and those who are not are removed. Let us resolve loving our neighbor into a spiritual activity, beholding love as the substance of all that is, no matter what the form may be. As we rise above our humanhood to a higher dimension of life in which we understand our neighbor to be pure spiritual being, God-governed, neither good nor bad, we are truly loving.

Love is the law of God. When we are in tune with divine love, loving whether it be friend or enemy, then love is a gentle thing bringing peace. But it is gentle only while we are in tune with it. It is like electricity. Electricity is very gentle and kind, giving light, warmth, and energy, as long as the laws of electricity are obeyed. The minute they are violated or played with, electricity becomes a double-edged sword. The law of love is as inexorable as the law of electricity.

Now let us be very clear on one point: We cannot harm anybody, and nobody can harm us. No one can injure us, but we injure ourselves by a violation of the law of love. The penalty is always upon the one who is doing the evil, never upon the one to whom it is done. The injustice we do to another reacts upon ourselves; the theft from another robs ourselves. The law of love makes it inevitable that the person who seems to have been harmed is really blessed. He has a greater opportunity to rise than ever before, and usually some greater benefit comes to him than he had ever dreamed possible; whereas the perpetrator of the evil deed is haunted by memories until that day comes when he can forgive himself. The whole proof that this is true is in the one word "Self." God is our Selfhood. God is my Selfhood and God is your Selfhood. God constitutes my being, for God is my life, my Soul, my spirit, my mind, and my activity. God is my Self. That Self is the only Self there is—my Self and your Self. If I rob your Self, whom am I robbing? My Self. If I lie about your Self, about whom am I lying? My Self. If I cheat your Self, whom do I cheat? My Self. There is only one Self, and that which I do to another, I do to my Self.

The Master taught this lesson in the twenty-fifth chapter of Matthew, when he said: "Inasmuch as ye have done it unto one of the least of these my brethren, ye have done it unto me." What I do of good for you, I am not doing for you at all; it is for my benefit. What I do of evil to you, will not hurt you, for you will find a way to recover from it; the reaction will be on me. We must come to the place where we actually believe and can say with our whole heart: "There is only one Self. The injustice that I am doing to another I am doing to myself. The lack of thoughtfulness that I show to another, I am showing to myself." In such recognition, the true meaning of doing unto others as we would have them do unto us is revealed.

God is individual being, which means that God is the only Self, and there is no way for any hurt or evil to enter to defile the infinite purity of the Soul of God, nor anything at which evil can strike or to which it can attach itself. When the Master repeated the age-old wisdom: "Therefore all things whatsoever ye would that men should do to you, do ye even so to them: for this is the law and the prophets," he was giving us a principle. Unless we do unto others as we would have others do unto us, we injure, not the others, but ourselves. In this present state of human consciousness, it is true that the evil thoughts, dishonest acts, and thoughtless words we inflict upon others do harm them temporarily, but always in the end it will be found that the injury was not nearly so great to them as it was to ourselves.

In the days to come, when men recognize the great truth that God is the Selfhood of every individual, the evil aimed at us from another will never touch us, but will immediately rebound upon the one who sends it. In the degree that we recognize God as our individual being, we realize that no weapon that is formed against us can prosper because the only I is God. There will be no fear of what man can do to us, since our Selfhood is God and cannot be harmed. As soon as the first realization of this truth comes to us, we no longer concern ourselves with what our neighbor does to us. Morning, noon, and night we must watch our thoughts, our words, and our deeds to make certain that we, ourselves, are not responsible for anything of a negative nature which would have undesirable repercussions.

This will not result in our being good because we fear

evil consequences. The revelation of the one Self goes far deeper than that: It enables us to see that God is our Self-hood, and that anything of an erroneous or negative nature which emanates from any individual has power only in the degree that we ourselves give it power. So it is that whatever of good or of evil we do unto others, we do unto the Christ of our own being. "Inasmuch as ye have done it unto one of the least of these my brethren, ye have done it unto me." In that realization, we shall see that this is the truth about all men, and that the only road to a successful and satisfying life is to understand our neighbor to be our Self.

The Master has instructed us specifically as to the ways in which we can serve our fellow man. He emphasized the idea of service. His whole mission was the healing of the sick, the raising of the dead, and the feeding of the poor. The moment that we make ourselves avenues for the out-flow of divine love, from that very moment, we begin serving each other, expressing love, devotion, and sharing, all in the name of the Father.

Let us follow the example of the Master and seek no glory for ourselves. With him, always, it was the Father who doeth the works. There is never any room for self-justifica-tion, or self-righteousness, or self-glorification in the perform-ance of any kind of service. Sharing with one another should not be reduced to mere philanthropy. Some people wonder why they find themselves left with nothing when they have always been so charitable. They come upon lean days because they believe that they have given of their own possessions; whereas the truth is that "the earth is the Lord's and the fullness thereof." If we express our love for our fellow man, realizing that we are giving nothing of ourselves, but all is of the Father, from whom every good and perfect gift comes, we shall then be able to give freely and discover that with all our giving there yet remain twelve baskets full left over. To believe that we are giving of our property, our time, or our strength reduces such giving to philanthropy and brings with it no reward. The true giving comes when giving is a recognition that "the earth is the Lord's," and that whether we give of our time or our effort, we are not giving of our own, but of the Lord's. Then are we expressing the love which is of God.

As we forgive, divine love is flowing out from us. As we pray for our enemies, we are loving divinely. Praying for our friends profiteth nothing. The greatest rewards of prayer come when we learn to set aside specific periods every day to pray for those who despitefully use us, to pray for those who persecute us, to pray for those who are our enemies— not only personal enemies because there are some people who have no personal enemies, but religious, racial, or national enemies. We learn to pray, "Father, forgive them; for they know not what they do." When we pray for our enemies, when we pray that their eyes be opened to the Truth, many times these enemies become our friends.

We begin this practice with our personal relationships. If there are individuals with whom we are not on harmonious terms, we find, as we turn within and pray that brotherly love and harmony be established between us, that instead of enemies, we come into a relationship of spiritual brotherhood with them. Our relationship with everybody then takes on a harmony and a heretofore unknown joy.

This is not possible as long as we feel antagonism toward anyone. If we are harboring within us personal animosity, or if we are indulging in national or religious hatred, prejudice, or bigotry, our prayers are worthless. We must go to God with clean hands in order to pray, and to approach God with clean hands, we must relinquish our animosities. Within ourselves, we must first of all pray the prayer of forgiveness for those who have offended us, since they know not what they do; and secondly, acknowledge within ourselves: "I stand in relationship to God as a son, and therefore, I stand in relationship to every man as a brother." When we have established that state of purity within ourselves, then we can ask the Father:

Give me grace; give me understanding; give me peace; give me this day my daily bread—give me this day spiritual bread, spiritual understanding. Give me forgiveness, even for those harmless trespasses which I have unwittingly committed.

The person who turns within for light, for grace, for understanding, and for forgiveness never fails in his prayers.

The law of God is the law of love, the law of loving our enemies—not fearing them, not hating them, but loving them. No matter what an individual does to us, we are not to strike back. To resist evil, to retaliate, or to seek revenge is to acknowledge evil as reality. If we resist evil, if we refute it, if we avenge ourselves, or if we strike back, we are not praying for them which despitefully use us and persecute us.

How can we say that we acknowledge good alone, God, as the only power, if we hate our neighbor or do evil to anyone? Christ is the true identity and to recognize an identity other than Christ is to withdraw ourselves from Christ-consciousness.

Love your enemies, bless them that curse you, do good to them that hate you, and pray for them which despitefully use you, and persecute you;

That ye may be the children of your Father which is in heaven: for he maketh his sun to rise on the evil and on the good, and sendeth rain on the just and on the unjust.

MATTHEW 5:44, 45

There is no other way to be the Christ, the Son of God. The Christ-mind has in it no criticism, no judgment, no condemnation, but beholds the Christ of God as the activity of individual being, as your Soul and mine. Human eyes do not comprehend this because as human beings, we are good and bad; but spiritually, we are the Sons of God, and through spiritual consciousness we can discern the spiritual good in each other. There is no room in spiritual living for persecution, hatred, judgment, or condemnation of any person or group of people. It is not only inconsistent, but hypocritical to talk about the Christ and our great love for God in one breath, and, in the next breath, speak disparagingly of a neighbor who is of a different race, creed, nationality, political affiliation, or economic status. One cannot be the child of God as long as he persecutes or hates anyone or anything, but only as he lives in a consciousness of no judgment or condemnation.

The usual interpretation of "judge not" is that we are not to judge evil of anyone. We must go much further than that; we dare not judge good of anyone either. We must be as careful not to call anyone good as we are not to call anyone evil. We should not label anyone or anything as evil, but likewise, we should not label anyone or anything as good. The Master said: "Why callest thou me good? there is none good but one, that is God." It is the height of egotism to say: "I am good; I have understanding; I am moral; I am generous; I am benevolent." If any qualities of good are manifesting through us, let us not call ourselves good, but recognize these qualities as the activity of God. "Son, thou art ever with me, and all that I have is thine." All the good of the Father is expressed through me.

One of the basic principles of The Infinite Way is that good humanhood is not sufficient to ensure our entry into the spiritual kingdom, nor to bring us into oneness with cosmic law. It is undoubtedly better to be a good human being than a bad one, just as it is better to be a healthy human being than a sick one; but achieving health or achieving goodness, in and of itself, is not spiritual living.

Spiritual living comes only when we have risen above human good and human evil and realize: "There are not good human beings or bad human beings. Christ is the only identity." Then we look out on the world and see neither good men and women nor bad men and women, but recognize Christ alone as the reality of being.

Therefore if thou bring thy gift to the altar, and there rememberest that thy brother hath ought against thee;

Leave there thy gift before the altar, and go thy way; first be reconciled to thy brother, and then come and offer thy gift.

MATTHEW 5:23, 24

If we are holding anyone in condemnation as a human being, good or bad, just or unjust, we have not made peace with our brother and we are not ready for the prayer of communion with the Infinite. We rise above the righteousness of the scribes and Pharisees only when we stop seeing good and evil, and stop boasting about goodness as if any of us could be good. Goodness is a quality and activity of God alone, and because it is, it is universal.

Let us never accept a human being into our consciousness who needs healing, employing, or enriching because if we do, we are his enemy instead of his friend. If there is any man, woman, or child we believe to be sick, sinning, or dying, let us do no praying until we have made peace with that brother. The peace we must make with that brother is to ask forgiveness for making the mistake of sitting in judgment on any individual because everyone is God in expression. All is God manifested. God alone constitutes this universe; God constitutes the life, the mind, and the Soul of every individual.

"Thou shalt not bear false witness against they neighbor" has a much broader connotation than merely not spreading rumors or indulging in gossip about our neighbor. We are not to hold our neighbor in humanhood. If we say, "I have a good neighbor," we are bearing false witness against him just as much as if we said, "I have a bad neighbor," because we are acknowledging a state of humanhood, sometimes good and sometimes bad, but never spiritual. To bear false witness against our neighbor is to declare that he is human, that he is finite, that he has failings, that he is something less than the very Son of God. Every time we acknowledge humanhood, we violate cosmic law. Every time we acknowledge our neighbor as sinful, poor, sick, or dead, every time we acknowledge him to be other than the Son of God, we are bearing false witness against our neighbor.

In the violation of that cosmic law, we bring about our own punishment. God does not punish us. We punish ourselves because if I say that you are poor, I virtually am saying that I am poor. There is only one I and one Selfhood; whatever truth I know about *you* is the truth about *me*. If I accept the belief of poverty in the world, that reacts upon me. If I say that you are sick or that you are not kind, I am accepting a quality apart from God, an activity apart from God, and in that way I am condemning myself because there is but one Self. Ultimately, I convict myself by bearing false witness against my neighbor and I am the one who suffers the consequences.

The only way to avoid bearing false witness against our neighbor is to realize that the Christ is our neighbor, that our neighbor is a spiritual being, the Son of God, just as we are. He may not know it; we may not know it; but the truth is: I am Spirit; I am Soul; I am consciousness; I am God expressed—and so is he, whether he is good or bad, friend or enemy, next door or across the seas.

In the Sermon on the Mount, the Master gave us a guide and a code of human conduct to follow while developing spiritual consciousness. The Infinite Way emphasizes spiritual values, a spiritual code, which automatically results in good humanhood. Good humanhood is a natural consequence of spiritual identification. It would be difficult to understand that the Christ is the Soul and the life of individual being, and then quarrel with our neighbor or slander him. We place our faith, trust, and confidence in the Infinite Invisible, and we do not take into consideration human circumstances and conditions. Then, when we do come to human circumstances or conditions, we see them in their true relationship. When we say, "Thou shalt love thy neighbor as thyself," we are not speaking of human love, affection, or friendliness; we are holding our neighbor in spiritual identity, and then we see the effect of this right identification in the human picture.

Many times we find it difficult to love our neighbor because we believe that our neighbor is standing between us and our good. Let me assure you that this is far from true. No outer influence for good or evil can act upon us. We ourselves release our good. To understand the full meaning of this requires a transition in consciousness. As human beings, we think that there are those individuals in the world who can, if they would, be good to us; or we think that there are some who are an influence for evil, harm, or destruction. How can this possibly be true if God is the only influence in our life—God, who is "closer . . . than breathing, and nearer than hands or feet"? The only influence is that of the Father within, which is always good. "Thou couldest have no power at all against me, except it were given thee from above."

When we realize that our life is unfolding from within our own being, we come to the realization that no one on earth has ever hurt us, and no one on earth has ever helped us. Every hurt that has ever come into our experience has been the direct result of our inability to behold this universe as spiritual. We have looked upon it with either praise or condemnation, and no matter which it was, we have brought a penalty upon ourselves. If we look back over the years, we could almost blueprint the reasons for every bit of discord that has come into our experience. In every case, it is the same thing—always because we saw somebody or something that was not spiritual.

Nobody can benefit us; nobody can harm us. It is what goes out from us that returns to bless or to condemn us. We create good and we create evil. We create our own good and we create our own evil. God does not do either: God *is*. God is a principle of love. If we are at-one with that principle, then we bring good into our experience; but if we are not at-one with that principle, we bring evil into our experience. Whatever is flowing out from our consciousness, that which is going forth in secret, is being shown to the world in outward manifestation.

Whatever emanates from God in the consciousness of man, individually or collectively, is power. What is it that emanates from God and operates in the consciousness of man but love, truth, completeness, perfection, wholeness— all of the Christ-qualities? Because there is only one God, one infinite Power, love must be the controlling emotion in the hearts and souls of every person on the face of the globe.

Now in contrast to that, are those other thoughts of fear, doubt, hate, jealousy, envy, and animality, which are probably uppermost in the consciousness of many of the people of the world. We, as truth-seekers, belong to a very small minority of those who have received the impartation that the evil thoughts of men are not power; they have no control over us. Not all the evil or false thinking on earth has any power over you or over me when we understand that love is the only power. There is no power in hate; there is no power in animosity; there is no power in resentment, lust, greed, or jealousy.

There are few people in the world who are able to accept the teaching that love is the only power and who are willing to "become as a little child." Those who do accept this basic teaching of the Master, however, are those of whom he said:

> . . . I thank thee, O Father, Lord of heaven and earth, that thou hast hid these things from the wise and prudent, and hast revealed them unto babes: even so, Father; for so it seemed good in thy sight.
> . . . Blessed are the eyes which see the things that ye see:
> For I tell you, that many prophets and kings have desired to see those things which ye see, and have not seen them; and to hear those things which ye hear, and have not heard them.
>
> LUKE 10:21, 23, 24

Once we accept this all-important teaching of the Master and our eyes see beyond the appearance, we shall consciously realize daily that every person in the world is empowered with love from on High, and that the love in his consciousness is the only power, a power of good unto you, unto me, and unto himself; but that the evil in human thought, whether it takes the form of greed, jealousy, lust, or mad ambition, is not power, is not to be feared or hated.

Our method of loving our brother as ourselves is in this realization: The good in our brother is of God and is power; the evil in our brother is not power, not power against us, and in the last analysis, not even power against him, once he awakens to the truth. To love our brother means to know the truth about our brother: to know that that in him, which is of God, is power and that in him, which is not of God, is not power. Then are we truly loving our brother. Centuries of orthodox teaching have instilled in all the peoples of the world a sense of separation so that they have developed interests separate and apart from one another and also apart from the world at large. When we master the principle of oneness, however, and this principle becomes a conviction deep within us, in that oneness the lion and the lamb can lie down together.

This is proved to be true through an understanding of

the correct meaning of the word "I." Once we catch the first perception of the truth that the *I* of me is the *I* of you, the Self of me is the Self of you, then we shall see why we have no interests apart from each other. There would be no wars, no conflicts of any kind, if only it could be made clear that the real being of everybody in the universe is the one God, the one Christ, the one Soul, and the one Spirit. What benefits one benefits another because of this oneness.

In that spiritual oneness, we find our peace with one another. If we experiment with this we shall quickly see how true it is. When we go to the market, we realize that everyone we meet is this same one that we are, that the same life animates him, the same Soul, the same love, the same joy, the same peace, the same desire for good. In other words, the same God sits enthroned within all those with whom we come in contact. They may not, at the moment, be conscious of this divine Presence within their being, but they will respond as we recognize It in them. In the business world, whether it is among our co-workers, our employers, or our employees, whether it is among competitors, or whether in management and labor relationships, we maintain this attitude of recognition:

I am you. My interest is your interest; your interest is mine, since the one life animates our being, the one Soul, the one Spirit of God. Anything we do for each other, we do because of the principle that binds us together.

A difference is immediately noticeable in our business relationships, in our relationships with tradespeople, and in our community relationships—ultimately, in national and international relationships. The moment that we give up our human sense of separateness, this principle becomes operative in our experience. It has never failed and it never will fail to bring forth rich fruitage.

Everyone is here on earth but for one purpose, and that

purpose is to show forth the glory of God, the divinity and the fullness of God. In that realization, we shall be brought into contact only with those who are a blessing to us as we are a blessing to them.

The moment we look to a person for our good, we may find good today and evil tomorrow. Spiritual good may come *through* you to me from the Father, but it does not come *from* you. You cannot be the source of any good to me, but the Father may use you as an instrument for Its good to flow through you to me. So, as we look at our friends or our family in this light, they become instruments of God, of God's good, reaching us through them. We come under grace by taking the position that all good emanates from the Father within. It may appear to come through countless different people, but it is an emanation of good, of God from within us.

What is the principle? "Love thy neighbor as thyself." In obeying this commandment we love friend and foe; we pray for our enemies; we forgive, though it be seventy times seven; we bear not false witness against our neighbor by holding him in condemnation; we judge not as to good or evil, but see through every appearance to the Christ-identity —the one Self which is your Self and my Self. Then can it be said of us:

. . . Come, ye blessed of my Father, inherit the kingdom prepared for you from the foundation of the world:

For I was an hungred, and ye gave me meat: I was thirsty, and ye gave me drink: I was a stranger, and ye took me in:

Naked, and ye clothed me: I was sick, and ye visited me: I was in prison, and ye came unto me.

Then shall the righteous answer him, saying, Lord, when saw we thee an hungred, and fed thee? or thirsty, and gave thee drink?

When saw we thee a stranger, and took thee in? or naked, and clothed thee?

Or when saw we thee sick, or in prison, and came unto thee?
And the King shall answer and say unto them, Verily I say
unto you, Inasmuch as ye have done it unto one of the least of
these my brethren, ye have done it unto me.

MATTHEW 25:34-40

CHAPTER VI

TO HIM THAT HATH

When the Master was called upon to feed the multitudes and the disciples told him that there were only a few loaves and fishes, he did not recognize that there was an insufficiency. No, he began with what was available and multiplied that, for he knew that "he that hath, to him shall be given; and he that hath not, from him shall be taken even that which he hath."

Scripture tells the story of the widow who fed Elijah. Even though she had only a "handful of meal in a barrel, and a little oil in a cruse," she did not say she had not enough to share, but first she made a little cake for Elijah before she baked one for her son and herself. "And the barrel of meal wasted not, neither did the cruse of oil fail." She had little, but she used what she had and let it flow out from her.

Day after day we are faced with the same question: What have we? If we are well-grounded in the letter of truth, the answer is clear and certain:

I have; all that God has, I have because "I and my Father are one." The Father is the source of all supply. In this relationship of oneness, I embody all supply. How, then, can I expect it to come to me from the outside? I must agree that I already have all that the Father has because of my oneness with the Father.

Are we that which receives, or are we that center from which the infinity of God flows out? Are we the multitudes who sat at the feet of the Master waiting to be fed, or are we the Christ feeding the unillumined? In the answer to that lies our degree of spiritual fulfillment. "I and my Father are one" means exactly what it says. We dare not ever look outside of our own being for our good, but we must ever look upon ourselves as that center from which God is flowing. It is the function of the Christ, or Son of God, to be the instrument as which the good of God pours out into the world:

I am that center through which God operates, and, therefore, I understand the nature of supply. Never will I attempt to demonstrate supply; never will I attempt to get supply. Since the activity of the Christ, Itself, is supply, then all I need to do is to let it flow. Since "I and my Father are one," and I am the Christ, or Son of God, I am that place through which God flows. Therefore, I can meet every demand that is made upon me in the recognition of have.

This marks a transition in consciousness from being a receiver of good to a realization that we are that point in consciousness through which the infinity of God's good flows to those not yet aware of their true identity.

From childhood, it has been instilled in us that we need certain people and certain things to make us happy. We are told repeatedly that we need money, home, companionship, family, vacations, automobiles, television sets, and all the paraphernalia considered essential to modern living. The spiritual life reveals clearly that God's grace is our sufficiency in all things. We do not need anything in this world except His grace. When we are tempted to believe that we need things, we should bring to our remembrance the correct letter of truth, which is that His grace is our sufficiency in all things. As we stand in this truth in the face of every appearance, one of these days a moment of transition comes, and with it, an inner conviction that all that we need is God. It is true that if we had God and everything in the world, we would not have any more than if we had God alone. If God is all-inclusive being, all is included in God.

Our relationship with God, our conscious oneness with God, constitutes our oneness with all spiritual being and idea. The moment we realize this, good begins to flow to us from outside, from sources all over the globe. Always it is the activity of God, not of a person. Every person comes bearing gifts because everyone is an instrument for the outflowing of God; but if we look to some specific person for our good, we block it. Wives who look to husbands, husbands who look to investments, and business people who look to the public are all looking amiss. The beginning of wisdom is the realization that the kingdom of God is within us and that it must flow out from us. We lose all sense of dependence on the world as we stand in the correct letter of truth and remember that His grace is our sufficiency in all things. Ultimately, this correct letter of truth registers in consciousness, and the Spirit takes over.

Life would become a miracle of unceasing joy and immeasurable abundance, if only we could abide in the consciousness of this truth of His grace as our sufficiency in all things:

Thy grace is sufficient for my every need, not Thy grace tomorrow, but Thy grace, since before Abraham was. Thy grace is my sufficiency unto the end of the world. Thy grace

of the past, present, and future is at this very instant my
sufficiency in all things.

Situations arise daily to tempt us to believe that we, or
our families, are in need of some form of good, either food,
housing, opportunity, education, employment, or rest; but to
all these things we respond: "Man shall not live by bread
alone, but by every word that proceedeth out of the mouth of
God," because His grace is our sufficiency in every circumstance.

Through the use of scriptural passages, we build such a
consciousness of the ever-presence of the Infinite Invisible
that although we continue to enjoy and appreciate everything
in the world of form, everything that exists as effect, yet never
again do we have the feeling that we need or require anything. Inasmuch as God's grace is our sufficiency, we do not
live by effect alone, but by every word of truth that has been
embodied in our consciousness and by every passage of truth
that we have made our own.

Every word of truth must be learned and made a part of
our consciousness so that it becomes flesh of our flesh and
bone of our bone, until the past, present, and future are all
bound up in the conscious realization of God's grace as our
sufficiency. In other words, our consciousness of truth is the
source, substance, activity, and law of our daily experience.

When we recognize God as the source of all good, God
as our sufficiency, and that people and circumstances are
but the avenue or instrument of our supply, we are likely to
have the experience of Moses with manna falling from the
sky, or Elijah with ravens bringing food, finding cakes baked
on the stones, or a widow sharing. Anything can happen, but
one thing is certain to happen, and that is abundance.

In every avenue or walk of life, it becomes necessary to
carry truth out into the world as an activity of consciousness. You may say that this is hard work, but it is much

harder than you think. That is why the Master called the Way straight and narrow. There were always multitudes coming to him to be fed, but there were never multitudes multiplying loaves and fishes. Healings can be brought forth through the work of teachers and practitioners, but unless we, ourselves, embody this truth in consciousness, we shall have lost our opportunity to achieve freedom from limitation here and now.

"He that hath, to him shall be given; and he that hath not, from him shall be taken even that which he hath." That sounds like a very heartless statement, but, nevertheless, it is the law, and an important principle of life. If we are faced with a problem and admit that we do not have enough understanding, enough experience, or enough supply to meet a particular demand made upon us, we have declared the little that we have. Very quickly that little will be taken from us because, in our admission of lack, we have done all that is necessary to impoverish ourselves; we have declared our own lack, and the only demonstration we can make is a perfect one. We shall demonstrate perfect and complete lack. Everyone who *desires* will make a perfect demonstration of *desire*. Only in the degree that he acknowledges fulfillment can he achieve fulfillment.

"To him that hath"! What do we have? Is there anyone who does not know one statement of truth? Then take that one statement and acknowledge, not that you lack, but that you *have*. Sit in the silence with that one statement and watch how rapidly another will come, followed by a third, fourth, fifth, and on—on into infinity. As many statements as you need will flow to you, because you will discover that it is not the truth you know that is coming to you, but the truth God knows. God is imparting His understanding and His truth to you. Your only responsibility is to open your consciousness and be receptive.

That which flows out is never from ourselves: It is from

the Father flowing through us, and the greater the demands that are made upon Him, the greater the flow. We find that illustrated in the cruse of oil which never ran dry; merely by lifting it up and beginning to pour, the flow of oil was continuous. We find the same phenomenon in the multiplication of loaves and fishes. By taking that which we have and using it, more keeps flowing and flowing. By acknowledging that we *have*, we shall demonstrate *have*. In the acknowledgment of God's wisdom, understanding, presence, and infinity within us, the flow begins. We block our own realization of harmony by claiming an insufficiency of truth under the false guise of humility. It is not our truth or the truth we know, but the truth God knows.

If we agree with Scripture, "Son, thou art ever with me, and all that I have is thine," and that we are joint-heirs with Christ to all the heavenly riches, we shall realize that nothing we have in the world is ours by virtue of our own strength or wisdom, but by virtue of sonship, by virtue of divinity, by virtue of being the child of God. In our divine sonship, how can we go about begging, asking, pleading, or expecting our good to come to us from other people? There is no consistency in that.

Let us agree that we are the branch, Christ is the vine— the invisible Presence within us—and God is the Godhead with which we are one. If we have a fruit tree, which at this moment is barren and has no fruit on it, we do not ask anybody to fasten peaches, pears, or apples on our barren fruit tree. We do not expect that one tree in the orchard is going to supply another tree, or that one branch will provide fruit for another branch. Each tree bears fruit from within itself. To a person who has never seen the miracle of a fruit tree, it must seem strange that from inside the tree, fruit comes forth through the branches. Reason would ridicule such a possibility. Here is an empty branch and here is an empty trunk; now how are peaches going to come up from inside the trunk and hang themselves on the branches? It may be a mystery, but the fact is that it is a regular phenomenon of nature.

It is incomprehensible to the human mind to say that our supply does not come from one another—that our neighbors, friends, or relatives do not provide for our needs—but that we, individually, through our contact with God receive our supply from within our own being. Just as the spider spins its web from within itself, so does our good unfold from within our own being.

"Son, all that I have is thine" is the correct letter of truth, but merely to know it intellectually will not change lack into abundance. This statement of truth provides the basis with which to meet every suggestion of limitation, but one day we no longer say it; we feel it, and in that moment, it becomes the law unto our experience. From then on, we no longer have to take thought for what we shall eat or drink or wherewithal we shall be clothed, because the law of divine inheritance has taken over. Our good comes to us at the right time without any human scheming. It does not mean that we do not give serious, conscientious thought to our work, but from now on we do this for the sake of the work and not to make a living. Whatever we do, we do because that is the work given us to do at this moment. We do the best that we can possibly do, but not for the purpose of making a living. Very soon we find that if we are not in the type of work that satisfies our Soul-sense, we are lifted out of what we are doing into something else. This will never happen, however, as long as we believe that our work is the source of our supply.

Once we realize "*have*," that "I and my Father are one, and all that the Father hath is mine," from that moment on, we find ways for that good to flow out from us. We cannot *get* love; we cannot *get* supply; we cannot *get* truth; we cannot *get* a home; we cannot *get* companionship. All of these things are embodied within us. We cannot *get* these things, but we *can* begin to pour; we *can* begin to multiply. *We* must make the beginning. Just the recognition of this principle may open the way for us to experience all good, but, on the other hand, it may be necessary for us consciously to open out specific ways for it to flow. If we need supply, we must begin expressing it, and there are many ways of doing that. People may give part of what they have to some charitable enterprise, or they may even make some unnecessary expenditure just to prove that they *have*.

Money is not the only way to start the flow. We can begin spending love, forgiveness, co-operation, and service. Any bestowal that is meant for God or God's children is a giving of oneself. This is the application of the principle that no good can come *to* us; good must flow out *from* us.

Is it not clear that the expectation of receiving good from any source outside of our own being would be the very attitude which would separate us from that good, but that a constant seeking within for greater opportunities to release the good already established in us, to let it flow, to express it, to share it, would open the windows of heaven? We should give because we *have*—give because we have an abundance, give because we have love and gratitude to overflowing. Gratitude is not related to an expectancy of what we may receive tomorrow. Gratitude is the sharing or expressing of joy for the good already received. It is a giving without a single sign, without a single trace of desire for a return. Any form of giving, whether it is the giving of the tangibles, such as money, food, or clothing, or the giving of the intangibles, such as forgiveness, understanding, consideration, kindness, generosity, love, peace, or harmony, should be because we have an abundance. Then comes the transformation in consciousness which reveals our Christhood.

Christhood never seeks to receive. There is no record in the entire New Testament of the Master's seeking health, wealth, recognition, reward, fame, payment, or gratitude.

The Christ shines; Its complete activity is that of shining. That is why the Christ is often referred to as the light. Light cannot receive anything: Light is a flowing; light is an expression; light is an outpouring. So is Christhood. It never has any desire to receive anything; It is Itself the infinity of God in individual expression. The moment an individual gives thought to the seeking of a return, he is in humanhood again; he is not in Christhood, because Christhood is the fullness of the Godhead bodily, made individually manifest.

Christhood is very much like integrity. Integrity is that which pours itself out, but does not look for a return. Integrity is not a quality of being that seeks a reward or a return. Integrity is a state of being for no other reason than being. So is Christhood. In achieving even a tiny measure of It, there is no longer a personal self which needs to be served. Christhood is a servant, not a master; It is that which bestows, gives, shares; but It has nothing to receive in return, because It already is the fullness of the Godhead bodily. That is what constitutes Christhood. As an individual expresses integrity, not for a return, but because it is the nature of his being, so it is that in Christhood one lives his life as an instrument through which God can pour Itself out in Its fullness.

The Hebrews were taught to share the first-fruits of their possessions by giving 10 per cent of their crops, cattle, herds, and goods to the temple. This is the practice of tithing, which has been interpreted to mean that if we give 10 per cent of our income for religious or charitable purposes, we are fulfilling the requirement of giving of our first-fruits. But there is a much wider, broader vision behind the idea of first-fruits. For example, if we were to give of our first-fruits to one another, it would mean that we would give of our spiritual vision to one another by consciously knowing the truth, by knowing God to be the source of individual being.

We give of our first-fruits to our friends and our relatives in the recognition of their true identity. Ultimately, we must do this for our enemies as well. The Master instructs us to pray for our enemies, because he says it does not profit us to pray for our friends. We must pray for our enemies and we must forgive. We must forgive those who abuse us, those who sin against us. This is not easy, but that does not make it any the less necessary, because it is through this practice that the Christ is born in us. To agree that each one of us is the instrument of the Christ of God, through which all blessings can flow out to this universe, brings the experience of the Christ to us.

Giving of our first-fruits is casting our bread upon the waters. Only the bread which we have cast upon the waters can return to us. We have no right to the bread which has been cast there by our neighbor. There is nothing in the world that has any way of returning to us except that which we place out in the world. The principle is that life is complete within us. As we permit it to flow out, it flows back to us. We have a right only to the bread of life that we place on the waters of life, because God has planted in us the completeness of Its own being. The bread we cast is the substance of life, that which sustains and maintains us. Our casting of bread upon the waters consists of knowing the truth about God as the Soul of this universe and as the mind, the life, and the Spirit of individual being. In that knowing, we would be casting spiritual bread upon the waters, and then eternal bread would be ours. Our realization of our oneness with God gives us the fullness of the Godhead bodily, and we are "heirs of God, and joint-heirs." Then it can begin to flow out from us.

The principle of abundance is: "*To him that hath, shall be given.*" Practice this principle by casting your bread upon the waters, giving freely of yourself and your possessions, knowing that what you are giving is God's, and that you are merely the instrument as which it flows out into the world. Never look for a return, but rest in quiet confidence in the assurance that within is the fountain of life, and *His* grace *is* your sufficiency in all things. In that certainty, born of an inner understanding of the letter of truth, you *have*. The cup of joy runs over, and all that the Father has flows forth into expression.

CHAPTER VII

MEDITATION

To him that hath shall be given . . . love the Lord thy God with all thy heart . . . love thy neighbor as thyself . . . I and my Father are one": These are important principles for any aspirant on the spiritual path. But how are these principles to be *realized*? It is one thing to state what *is*, but it is another thing to achieve it or accomplish it. Granted that there is this Father within of whom Jesus spoke, this Christ through which we can do all things, how then do *we* individually achieve the experience of the Christ, that is, how do we bring that divine Presence into our affairs? That is the important point.

In The Infinite Way, the age-old theme of meditation and inner communion is emphasized, the practice of which enables a person to come out and be separate—whether he is sitting reverently in a church, whether he has retired to some quiet corner of his own home, or whether he is basking in the sunshine of a garden—and, forgetting the things of this world, to turn within and make contact with his inner forces, with that which we call God, the Father within, the Christ

93

The experience of the Christ is a present possibility; the way to that experience is through meditation.

Far too many aspirants to the spiritual way of life know the letter of truth and are satisfied to stop there. "I and my Father are one" is the correct letter of truth. Does repeating these words or does an intellectual knowledge of them help us in any way? How often do we say: "I am God's perfect child; I am spiritual; I am divine"; and then find that we are just as poor as we were before, or in just as much trouble. These are only statements. It is similar to sitting in a dark room and saying over and over again, "Electricity gives light." That is a correct statement, but we shall still be sitting in the dark until, by turning on the switch, a connection is made with the source of electricity. So nothing is going to happen to us, regardless of how many affirmations of truth we know or repeat, unless we attain the consciousness of that truth and realize our oneness with our Source. Meditation is that way.

The kingdom of God is within us; the place whereon we stand is holy ground. Wherever we are, God is, in church or out of church. The Master says, "Ye shall neither in this mountain, nor yet at Jerusalem, worship the Father." God is not found in places; God is found in consciousness. God is where we are because "I and My Father are one." We cannot escape from God.

Whither shall I go from thy spirit? or whither shall I flee from thy presence?

If I ascend up into heaven, thou art there: if I make my bed in hell, behold, thou art there.

If I take the wings of the morning, and dwell in the uttermost parts of the sea;

Even there shall thy hand lead me, and thy right hand shall hold me.   PSALM 139:7–10

Where we are, God is; where God is, we are because we are one, inseparable and indivisible:

I will never leave you, nor forsake you. I will never leave you nor forsake you wherever you are or whatever you are— Hindu, Jew, Christian, Moslem, atheist. It is My nature to be the very heart and soul of your being. Neither your stupidities nor your sins can come between you and Me.

You may temporarily separate yourself from Me, that is, you may think you have separated yourself from Me, and you certainly can separate yourself from the benefit of my Presence, but that does not mean that I have left you. You will find that at any moment, night or day, whether you make your bed in hell or in heaven, whether you walk through the valley of the shadow of death, at any time you like, you may turn and you will find that I am walking beside you. I am the everlasting arms underneath you. I am the cloud by day and the pillar of fire by night. I am that which sets a table before you in the wilderness. If you are hungry, I am the ravens that come bringing you food. I am the widow sharing a little cake and a cruse of oil.

I will never leave you. I will be manna to you in your desert experience. I will be that which opens the Red Sea for you, if no other way opens. I AM THAT which I AM, forever and forever. I have been That unto eternity and will be That, for I am I in the midst of you. Whithersoever thou goest, I will go.

God is not found up in heaven—not in pilgrimages, places, or persons. God is to be found within us. The very moment that we can agree inwardly that this is true, we have accomplished half of our life's journey toward the experience of heaven on earth; the other half remains. Now we know *where* the kingdom of God is, but *how* do we attain the realization of it? The men and women who searched for the Holy Grail, their symbol of the kingdom of God, spent a lifetime only to discover that it was a mistake to seek outside for that which was already within them. They returned from their search exhausted physically, financially, and mentally, discouraged by the failure of their mission. Then all of a sudden, they looked around and found the golden chalice hanging up in the tree, or they heard the bluebird caroling its message of joy—right in their own home all of the time. That is what happens when we come to the realization that the kingdom of God is within us. One half of the journey is then accomplished.

Hundreds of books have been written on this subject, but those that have been written out of the depths of experience all agree that the presence of God can only be realized when the senses are stilled, when we have settled down into an atmosphere of expectancy, of hope, and of faith. In this state of relaxation and peace, we wait. That is all we can do, just wait. We cannot bring God to us for God is already here, in this inner stillness, in this quietness and confidence.

Meditation is an invitation for God to speak to us or to make Himself known to us; it is not an attempt to reach God, since God is omnipresent. The Presence already is. The Presence always is, in sickness or in health, in lack or in abundance, in sin or in purity; the presence of God always and already is. We are not seeking to reach God, but rather to achieve such a state of stillness that the awareness of God's presence permeates us.

We have been trained to pray with our thinking mind as if God could be reached through thought. God can never be reached with or through thought. No one can ever reach God with the mind; no one can ever reach God with conscious thinking: God can only be reached through a receptive state of consciousness. We never know when God will speak to us, but of this we may be assured: If we live in meditation, giving sufficient periods to maintaining our contact with the Presence, we shall be under God's government, and at any moment that there is a necessity or a need, God will speak to us.

It is within us that the contact must be made. Until it has been made, the Spirit of God in man is merely a promise; the Christ is but a word or a term. It must become an experience, but until it does become an experience, the question may well be raised: Is there a Spirit within man? Is the Christ real? Withinness is the secret.

Centuries and centuries of looking for our good in the other person's garden, centuries and centuries of thinking that our good must come to us by might and by power or by the sweat of our brow, have separated us from the depths of this withinness, so that it is as if there were a great wall between us and that Christ. It takes constant turning within to tear away the veil of illusion, that middle-wall of partition which seems to separate us. How speedily we shall pierce the veil has no relationship to our human goodness or to the depth of our sins: It has a relationship only to the depth of our desire to make the contact. When we make that contact, not only are our sins forgiven, but they are healed. It is not a question of a person's first becoming good before he can come under God's grace. No, it operates in reverse order: Let God's grace touch a person, and it will make him good. The Spirit within will change the outer life; the inner grace will appear outwardly.

If we persist in the realization: "The kingdom of God is within me; the place whereon I stand is holy ground; Son thou art ever with me, and all that I have is thine"; and if we remember to do this two or three times a day, every day, one of these fine days something happens to us: An experience takes place—it may be a feeling of warmth; it may be a feeling of release; it may be a voice in the ear; but it is something that takes place within, and we, within ourselves, know that we have had the visitation of the Christ. Then we know that we have experienced the annunciation and the conception of the Christ; the Christ in us is awakened, and from then on we are able to say:

"I can do all things through Christ," not through my human wisdom, not through my muscles, not because I know
a lot of words and have read many books; but through
Christ, I can do all things. The Christ within me strengtheneth me; the Christ within me is a Presence that goes before
me to make the crooked places straight.

This will no longer be a series of quotations: This will be an
experience.

This inner experience will become the substance of our
outer experience. It can pour out of our mouth as a message;
it can pour out of our home as happiness; it can pour out
of our business as success; but it must be a realized Christ, a
risen Christ; it must be a Christ felt in consciousness. It must
touch us; It must warm us; It must illumine us.

Then we can rest, but not for too long, because the mes-
merism of the world forces itself upon us, and six hours later,
sensational newspaper headlines and radio news impinge
on our consciousness, and the Christ begins to slip into the
background. So we learn to sit down again and renew ourselves, fill ourselves with the realization of this presence of
the Christ, and six hours later we do it again.

The day comes when this realization of the Christ is an
hourly practice, and finally, it becomes unnecessary at all,
because at that stage, the Christ takes over and lives our life,
and no further conscious effort is necessary. But before this
stage of development is reached, conscious effort is necessary to achieve that mind "which was also in Christ Jesus,"
to achieve the realization of the presence of the Christ; and
this conscious effort requires hours and hours of meditation
and contemplation. It is in these hours of meditation and
contemplation that we open ourselves to the Christ. Words
become unnecessary; thoughts become unnecessary. Thoughts
now come to us from the Within. God's Word is spoken to

us, uttered within us. We are no longer voicing words, but the Word.

How deep is our desire for the realization of God? How can we gauge the depth of our love for God? The answer is very simple: How much time and attention are we willing to give to sitting down in the silence until we feel God's presence? That determines how much love for God we have. If we do not have the time, if we do not have the patience, if we do not have the willingness to give our whole heart and soul and mind to the realization of this presence of the Christ, we do not have sufficient love for God. It is similar to having a mother living in a distant place. How hard are we willing to struggle, how great a sacrifice are we willing to make to obtain the money to visit her or to send her the money to provide for her comfort? That will determine how much love we have. We should use the same kind of measuring rod in determining our love for God. How much are we willing to sacrifice of time or effort for reading, study, or whatever may be necessary to arouse that sleeping, invisible Christ? That is the measure of our love.

When we arrive at that place where we have no fewer than four periods of meditation a day, we are beginning to obey Paul's injunction to "pray without ceasing." The mystics revealed that in quietness and in stillness is our strength. In quietness and in stillness we find God, not in outside worship.

Jesus went a step further and told us that we must pray in secret: We must enter the inner sanctuary, close the door, and pray where men cannot see us. When we are alone, there is an opportunity for something to take place that can never take place in public. Why? Because when we are in public, the ego is on display. We cannot be ourselves, even in the presence of our loved ones. Anything that tends to display the ego destroyes our spiritual integrity. The more secret and sacred we keep our relationship to God, never making an open display of it at any time, the more power there is in it.

The ego must be destroyed to make way for the one Ego, our Christhood. As human beings, we have a selfhood of our own which we like to glorify. The whole teaching of Jesus was the destruction of the personal ego: "The words that I speak unto you I speak not of myself: but the Father that dwelleth in me, he doeth the works. . . . My doctrine is not mine but his that sent me." He overcame his ego and left a blueprint for us to follow: Pray in secret. He went even further and said: "When thou doest alms, let not thy left hand know what thy right hand doeth . . . and thy Father, which seeth in secret, himself shall reward thee openly." Every time we make our charities and benevolences a matter of public notice, every time we pray in public to be seen of men, every time we give expression to our religious convictions in public, we are glorifying our own ego, trying to show forth how much we do or how much we know. We forget that our Father, which seeth in secret, Himself shall reward us openly.

There is a great spiritual mystery in all of this. It is a very strange thing that as we draw closer and closer to God, and the more that we keep everything locked up within ourselves, the greater is our spiritual unfoldment. When it is a secret deep within us, God, in His own way, makes it known outwardly to those who may have any interest in knowing about our benevolences or our relationship to God.

The secret of meditation is silence: no repetitions, no affirmations, no denials—just the acknowledgment of God's allness, and then the deep, deep silence which announces God's presence. The deeper the silence, the more powerful is the meditation. The things that are holy, keep holy; keep them sacred and keep them secret. There is nothing of a sacred nature that we need to share with anyone. Everyone is free to search for God in his own way and must himself make the effort to find that for which he is seeking. There is no occasion for sharing the deeper things, for sharing the more sacred things in our relationship with God, because each one is free to go and do likewise. The deep things and the sacred things must be hidden within our own consciousness. The more we keep secret and sacred within us, the greater is the power.

Continuous inner meditation, continuous reaching toward the center of our being, will eventually result in the experience of the Christ. In that moment, we discover the mystery of spiritual living: We do not have to take thought for what we shall eat, what we shall drink, or wherewithal we shall be clothed; we do not have to plan; we do not have to struggle. Only Christ can live our life for us, and we meet the Christ within ourselves in meditation. The degree to which we attain the experience or activity of the Christ, the presence of the Spirit of God in us, determines the degree of individual unfoldment.

When, through meditation, we have attained this realization of the Spirit of God, and abide in it, retire into the center of our being, day in and day out, so that we never make a move without Its inner assurance, the activity of the Christ feeds us, supplies us, enriches us, heals us, and brings us into the fullness of life. Then, of a certainty, we know, "I am come that they might have life, and that they might have it more abundantly."

CHAPTER VIII

THE RHYTHM OF GOD

A person who lives by meditation is never again alone, and neither is he ever again entirely a part of this world. If he is faithful in practicing the Presence, within a few months he will find himself in the contemplative mood most of the time. Contemplating God and the invisible things of God, he becomes so one with It that there is no place where God leaves off and he begins. That which a person continuously dwells upon, that which he embraces in his consciousness, is that with which he ultimately becomes one. It is that continuous state of oneness which enabled the Master to say, "Thou seest me, thou seest the Father that sent me, for I and my Father are one."

Everything good must come into the experience of the Sons of God. Who are the Sons of God? Are we? Not until the Spirit of the Lord is upon us—"if so be that the spirit of God dwell in you, then are ye the sons of God," and only then are we subject to the laws of God. If we walk out of our homes without the inner awareness that the Spirit of the

Lord is upon us, we are walking out into the world as human beings without any law of God to uphold us; we are human beings subject to human laws—laws of accident, contagion, disease, and death. We have neglected the opportunity of admitting a divine influence into our experience, and our attitude virtually is, "I can live this day all right under my own power; I can take care of this day myself without any help from God," instead of making God the activity of the day and thereby establishing ourselves in the rhythm of God:

Father, this is Your day, the day which You have made. You made the sun to rise; You have given light and warmth to the earth; You have given us the rains and the snows; the seasons of the year are Yours, "seedtime and harvest, cold and heat, summer and winter, and day and night." This is Your day.

You created me; I am Yours. You created me in the womb from the beginning. Use me this day, for as the heavens declare the glory of God and the earth showeth forth Your handiwork, so must I show forth the glory of God. This day let me glorify God. This day, let God's will be made manifest in me. This day, let God's grace flow from me and through me to all those whom I meet.

Some other time, during that brief pause for inner communion in the early morning hours, these words may come:

Father, it is Thy intelligence that I need today—not my limited wisdom, but Thy infinite wisdom. This day, I need all the love with which Thou canst fill me. Give me Thy wisdom and Thy love in full measure.

Such a meditation springs from a deep humility, a great humbling of the spirit which is willing to admit, "Father, without Thee I can do nothing; without Thee, I can be nothing; without Thee, I am nothing."

It may be that the day holds serious problems which must be surmounted and which are beyond our ability or understanding, or beyond our financial capacity to meet, or there may be difficult decisions to be made. The answer does not lie in any personal ability we may or may not have, or in our material resources, but in contacting the infinite storehouse within: "He performeth the thing that is appointed for me. . . . The Lord will perfect that which concerneth me." To enter our inner sanctuary and pray, not asking for anything, but recognizing our divine sonship and dwelling on the promises of inspired scriptural passages, fills us with a confidence which we carry with us throughout the day and which is adequate to prevail over any and every obstacle which we may encounter:

Father, I have great tasks today that are beyond my understanding and beyond my strength, and so I must rely on You to perform that which is given me to do. You have said that You are ever with me and all that You have is mine. Grant me the assurance today that Your love is with me, that Your wisdom guides me, and that Your presence upholds me.

Your grace is my sufficiency in all things. Your grace! I am satisfied, Father, to know that Your grace is with me. That is all I ask because that grace will be made tangible as manna falling from the sky, as a cruse of oil that never runs dry, or as loaves and fishes that keep ever multiplying. Whatever my need, Your grace provides for it this day.

Just that much is enough to start us on our day, not as the son of man, but as the Son of God.

A Presence abides in us, a transcendental Presence which cannot be described, but which is recognized in meditation. There is no greater gift that can come to any man or woman than the unswerving conviction that God cares for us, but no one can have this assurance who neglects the continuous, conscious realization of the presence of God. If the Word abides in us, we shall bear fruit richly. God is glorified in the fruitage of our lives, and in no other way is God glorified. In proportion as we live in this Word and let it live in us, do we experience a harmonious, fruitful, human life. True, there may be problems, but what of it? No one is promised complete immunity from the discords of life while he is on earth living a human life. Problems must inevitably arise, but they can only be a blessing because it is through these problems that we rise higher in consciousness and through that rising, harmony is brought into our daily life.

The experiences that come to us when we live in obedience to the inner voice are miracles of beauty and joy. Let us not be afraid to follow that voice even if at first we are so poorly attuned to it that we do not hear it correctly. Many people go through life accomplishing nothing because they are unwilling to do anything for fear of making a mistake. There is no need to be afraid of mistakes or even of failures. Any mistakes which may be made by a person who is obedient to the still small voice will be few, and they will not be sufficiently serious to be irretrievable; he can quickly pick himself up again and soon be wholly immersed in the Spirit. Mistakes are not fatal; not one is forever: Success is forever, but failure is only for a day.

If we make contact with the kingdom of God within us, we shall be living through God the rest of our days. Then spiritual sonship—God expressing Itself as individual Selfhood—will be revealed on earth. God formed us to manifest Itself on earth, to show forth Its glory, and that is our destiny. God planted His infinite abundance in the midst of us. Nothing need come to you or to me, but everything must flow out from us. And by what means? By that Presence, that Presence which heals, supplies, multiplies, and teaches. That Presence will perform every legitimate function of life, but It is only active in our life as we dedicate and consecrate ourselves to periods of meditation. Devotion and consecration are necessary to give us sufficient purpose so that we remember a dozen times a day to make no move without the realized Presence, or at least without an acknowledgment of It.

There are ample opportunities in any person's day for acknowledging the Presence. It is not too difficult to develop the habit of waiting for a second at every door we open or close to realize:

God is just as much on the other side of this door as He is on this side. There is no place where I can go today where the presence of God is not. Wherever I am, God is.

We can pause before eating to remember that we do not live by bread alone, but by every word that proceedeth out of the mouth of God. Therefore, as we contemplate the food upon the table, we can silently express gratitude for the Source of that food, for That which brought it to us: "Thy grace hath set my table."

There is not a moment of the day when a spiritually alert person cannot find some reason to say, "Thank you, Father." Often there may be nothing for which to thank God except perhaps that the sun is shining, but even that is an acknowledgment of the Presence. Sometimes, when we are faced with frustrating or disturbing circumstances, we may wonder how we can praise God, but if we are awake in spiritual sonship, we can always find ways to acknowledge God. This continuous practice of the Presence, acknowledging God in all our ways, providing ample periods for sitting in the silence, and waiting for an inner feeling that the Spirit of God is moving, makes God the governing, maintaining, and sustaining principle of our entire experience. The real prayer of spiritual understanding is a prayer that God's gift of Himself may be given to us.

Infinity is within us at this and at every moment: all spiritual wisdom, all divine grace, eternality, and immortality—all of these are embodied within us at this and at every single moment. Let us begin to show forth this infinity. How? Begin to pour. Search around in your spiritual house, your consciousness, and see if you cannot find some biblical passage, some mite of love to express to someone, or a few drops of forgiveness. Find something in your house. Begin to let the few drops of oil you find there flow silently, secretly, and sacredly. Keep them flowing, and as you do, be receptive to what is unfolded from within. Do not attempt to make up statements or thoughts. Wait patiently in a relaxed state of receptivity for them to come to you. Soon a second idea will be added to the original thought. Contemplate both of them. Dwell upon their meaning; dwell upon their possible effect in your life or in the life of another. As you ponder these two ideas, sometimes gently, sometimes explosively, a third thought comes, something which you had not thought about before. And where are these ideas coming from? From within you. Remember they have always been there, but now you are letting them out. Within that Withinness is the storehouse that is your individual storehouse, yet it is infinite because it is God. The kingdom of God is within you, and in meditation you are drawing on it.

If there is not enough love in your life, it is only because you are not loving enough, and that means that you are not tapping the infinite source of love within your own being. Let that love flow out: Love this world; love the sun, the moon, and the stars; love the plants and the flowers; love all the people. Let the love flow. That love which flows out from the infinite storehouse within you will be the bread of life which will come back to you.

Let truth flow out from you into this world. The more truth you release, the more truth you will have. You are the instrument through which God's truth is flowing out into consciousness. You do not know where this truth is going or whom it is blessing. You do not know who is feeling the love that is welling up within you, and it is not important that you should know because it is not your love; it is God's love. You are but the instrument through which it is flowing. Always begin your meditation by realizing that infinity lies within you, that you are seeking nothing to come to you; you are never seeking to get, to acquire, or to achieve; you are seeking only to let God's grace flow through you, the instrument, the Son of God.

Perhaps someone is looking to you for spiritual blessings. Do not begin by believing that you have not enough understanding or have not read enough books or have not had sufficient experience to help him. Begin with the two drops of oil you already have, and you do that by knowing the truth, not about the person, but about God:

How much truth do I know about God? I know that God is omnipresent, and that therefore, all God's presence and all God's power are flowing through me. Where God is, there can be nothing but good; there cannot be sin, disease, death, lack, or limitation. In God's presence, is the allness of good.

What else do I know about God? God is the only power. If God is the only power, there are no powers other than God; there are no negative powers on earth so there can be no power in this condition confronting me. God is the only life, life eternal and immortal without sin or disease, without blemish. God's life is perfect. God is love, and that love enfolds me. God's love is my protection, sustaining and maintaining me.

This is the way healing work is done: Go within; get quiet; become still until the peace that passeth understanding descends.

True spiritual healing is not something that takes place in the body or in one's affairs; it takes place in the consciousness of the individual as the soul is opened. It is a regeneration more than it is a healing. Everything embraced within consciousness—body, business, home—responds as the Soul is opened to the light of truth and to the activity of God acting as individual consciousness.

Actually, there is no spiritual healing apart from spiritual living, and there can be no spiritual living apart from the experience of God. God must be experienced; God must be communed with in our inner being. The Infinite Invisible which we call God and our individual identity which we call the Son are one. It is within us that a point of contact must be made so that an absolute conviction of this divine Presence can come to us. That conviction can only well up from within; and as this Spirit of God fills us, we feel a sense of peace, a deep breath within us, a release as of a weight removed; and then we go about our normal, daily life, serene, secure, resting in the bosom of the Father, because now God, the Son, has God, the Father, with him.

God is not a healer of disease; *God is an infinity of being.* God is Spirit, and beside God there is nothing else. God's grace removes every obstacle from our path because the light of truth reveals that there never was power in the so-called obstacle. When we find our inner peace, we shall find that Omnipotence, omnipresent, is governing us, and all of the things which we feared—people or conditions—automatically disappear because of their nothingness. That is the miracle of spiritual teaching: It is not truth over error; it is not God over evil; it is not some great big God that does something to some even greater and more terrifying evil. A spiritual teaching is a revelation of God as infinite, individual being —as Spirit, omnipotent, omniscient, omnipresent—beside which there is no other. In that realization, darkness disappears, and light comes in.

"He uttered his voice, the earth melted." If we become so proficient in the practice of the Presence that we can sit quietly with our attention focused on the Within, the still small voice will thunder, and the whole earth of evil will melt and fade out of our experience. It may come as an actual voice; it may come as a vision; but neither is necessary: Only one thing is necessary and that is to wait until there is a stirring or a feeling which is our assurance that God has uttered His voice. When that occurs, we shall find that discord is replaced by harmony, sickness gives way to health, and the people we meet are no longer human beings but children of God. As we contemplate God's presence, grace, and power, God utters His voice and the whole world of discord disappears:

Closer to me than breathing is my God, the All-Presence and the only Presence, beside whom there is no other presence. "The Lord is my light and my salvation; whom shall I fear? the Lord is the strength of my life; of whom shall I be afraid?"

What, then, is this discord that is claiming my attention, that I am fearing? Is it a person? No, God is the Father of all: "Call no man your father upon the earth: for one is your Father, which is in heaven." Therefore, all men are spiritual, endowed only with the qualities of God. God made all that was made and He called it good. In the beginning is only God. Has anything been added to God? Has anything been added to God's universe? No, and in that recognition, I cannot be hynotized into seeing or believing that which is unlike God. God is the only creative principle of man. All that He creates is created in His own image and likeness, in the image and likeness of perfection.

The Father within me is the only power operating in this universe; the Father within me is the only power operating in this room; the Father within me is the only power operating within my own being. There is only God-being, the power of God which flows out into this world, blessing all whom it reaches, friend and foe alike.

"He uttered his voice, the earth melted"—the discord disappears. The inharmony and the person melt into His

image and likeness. This person who was disturbing me, where is he now? He is not here; he is risen; he is risen out of the tomb, no longer the man of flesh, but the child of God. In the stillness, when I have silenced all human judgments as to good or evil, "a child is born," the realization of the Christ takes place, and "whereas I was blind, now I see." I behold the vision infinite—God, the Father; and God, the Son.

God is maintaining and sustaining Its own life which is my life, the life of individual being, and God is maintaining that life now—not at some future time, but now. This body is the body that God gave me, a spiritual, eternal, and immortal body. God keeps my body in Its everlasting perfection. God is a continuous and eternal state of divine being, and that Being is my individual being, for "I and my Father are one." My body is an instrument for the activity of God, a fitting vehicle to show forth His glory. God is the very strength of my bones; God is the health of my countenance; God is my fortress and my high-tower, my safety and my security.

The earth showeth forth His handiwork; the heavens declare His glory. How can the heavens—the sun, the moon, and the stars—show forth that glory, and not man, who was given dominion over the sun, moon, and stars? Man shows forth the fullness of the Godhead bodily, not by struggling and battling to become that fullness, but only as he relaxes and lets the rhythm of God fulfill Itself in him. God's work is a complete work; man's work is to rest in it:

God in the midst of me is mighty, and because God is in the midst of me, I need nothing; I lack nothing. Of myself, I have no ability; I have no understanding of my own, but God's understanding is infinite. "He that is within me performeth that which is appointed for me. . . . He that is within me is greater than he that is in the world." I become

*the willing instrument of God, and through me, He utters
His voice and the earth melteth.*

I seek nothing for myself; I seek only to be used as an instrument to bring light to those still in darkness. I do not
use Truth, but I permit Truth to use me. I let Truth flow
through me to the nations of the world who are still seeking
what they shall eat and what they shall drink and wherewithal they shall be clothed; but I live, not by bread alone,
but by every word that proceedeth out of the mouth of God.
Every truth that comes into my consciousness is the length
of my days, my daily supply, and my wisdom and understanding. All I need or ever shall need is to hear the still small
voice within me and rest in the rhythm of God.

God's grace flows out into this world as an invisible Presence and as an invisible Power of blessing through me. I am
that center through which that grace is bestowed upon the
world—my world, God's instrument through which the divine wisdom, the bread of life, the wine of life, and the
water of life are reaching mankind. The nations of the world
seek bread, food, clothing, and housing, but "not ye, my disciples"—not I; I seek only the kingdom of God and I let God's
grace flow through me.

The Spirit of God in me is the Christ. Its function is to
heal, raise the dead, open the eyes of the blind—the materially and spiritually blind—and illumine human consciousness. "My peace," the Christ-peace, is given unto me and
through me to the world. That is the function of the light
that is pouring through me. The truth I am becomes the
bread of life to this world which does not yet know its own
identity. I, my divine Consciousness, become the wine and
the water. This light which I am becomes the light of the
world to the unillumined and my presence a benediction.

There is an eternal rhythm in the universe—"seedtime and
harvest, cold and heat, summer and winter, and day and
night . . . to everything there is a season, and a time to

every purpose under the heaven." We become one with that eternal purpose and rest in the rhythm of God as we contemplate the eternal flow of God's grace. The rhythm of the universe flows through us:

The heavens declare the glory of God; and the firmament sheweth his handiwork. Day unto day uttereth speech, and night unto night sheweth knowledge. . . . Let the words of my mouth, and the meditation of my heart, be acceptable in thy sight, O Lord, my strength, and my redeemer.

PSALM 19:1, 2, 14

CHAPTER IX

A MOMENT OF CHRISTHOOD

The correct letter of truth necessary for spiritual unfoldment is embodied in the principles as set forth in the foregoing chapters: Love God with all your heart, acknowledging that God is the only power and that there is no power in any effect; love your neighbor as yourself by refraining from all judgment as to good or evil, by forgiving seventy times seven, and by praying for your enemies; recognize the infinite nature of individual being, the corollary of which is that there is only one Self; begin to pour, in the realization that to him that hath shall be given; demonstrate God and not things; meditate on God and the things of God; and live only in this moment, which is the only moment there is.

A full realization of any one of these principles, living and working with it, day after day and week after week, would be sufficient to transform our experience and usher us into the kingdom of heaven. Instead of attempting to grasp the full meaning of truth in the short span of a day or a week, with one reading of this or of any other book, we should begin working with some one principle and take that principle into meditation daily for at least a month, dwelling on it until its inner meaning is revealed, and it becomes "the spirit that quickeneth," and then observe to what extent our words and acts are in harmony with it. Thus it becomes bone of our bone and flesh of our flesh.

Many times we let the pressure of the world rob us, not only of our peace, but of the time in which to have these quiet periods of renewal which work the transformation in our lives. If we are sincere in our desire to experience God, we shall make it a matter of decision to let nothing interfere with our firm resolve and steadfast purpose. Most of us know people who have already discovered the way to do this. These people are able to accomplish a tremendous amount of work and yet never seem to be pressed for time, but always, even in the midst of the most harassing circumstances, maintain a gentle tranquillity and a never-failing equanimity. They move in and out of confusion and withstand outside pressure with a quiet poise and an unruffled calm. What is their secret? How have they developed this ability?

There is a simple practice by which a considerable measure of this peace can be achieved, if persisted in day in and day out. It is by developing a consciousness of nowness, a state of todayness. This state of nowness is achieved by consciously training ourselves to live only in this minute, by recognizing, first of all, that we do not live on yesterday's manna. Since we live only on the manna as it falls today, our dependence is only on that which comes to us today and not on anything that was due from yesterday or was carried over from last month. We do not waste time thinking about past obligations people may owe us, nor about past hurts or wrongs they may have committed.

Our responsibility is only for this day and for this moment. Whatever demand is made upon us, let us fulfill it this moment. If a call comes to us for help, let us not wait until tonight to give the help, but answer the call at the moment it comes. If there is correspondence to be handled, it must be answered this day so that the next morning we come to our work and our day with a clear desk. It is surprising how much spare time we have during the day when we take care of everything as it is presented to us. Most of us never have free days because we are always attempting to finish work which has accumulated from yesterday and the day before, work which should have been done the day it was given us to do.

This practice of nowness develops a consciousness which is never pressed from the outside because there is nothing to do except what is at hand this minute. Living in this consciousness, we are never worried about supply, nor about any obligation due tomorrow. There is only today; there is only this hour of today; there is only this moment of today. Then there develops in us—*we* do not do it—*It*, the Christ of our being, develops in us a sense of peace, a sense of quiet so that we hear within us the words: "I can of mine own self do nothing. It is the Father within me that doeth the works. . . . I can do all things through Christ. I live, yet not I, but Christ liveth in me."

When "Christ liveth in me," when Christ lives my life for me, no demands are ever made upon *me*; every demand is a demand upon the Christ. The Father within can accomplish more in twelve seconds than we can in twelve hours. Let us be willing to be called upon for anything in this world, without resentment, without rebellion, without feeling that it is too much for us to do, or that too much is being asked of us. It may be too much for John or Mary or Henry to do, but it is never too much for the Christ.

There is only this moment—a moment of Christhood. We cannot live yesterday. No one has it within his ability to live yesterday and no one can live tomorrow. There is only one time in which we can live, and that is now, in this instant; it is what we are, in this instant, that constitutes our life.

In Isaiah we read, ". . . though your sins be as scarlet they shall be as white as snow." In the same vein, the Master said to the thief on the cross, "Today shalt thou be with me in paradise." These examples are indicative of but one point, and that is that we live in a constant state of nowness. Yesterday does not exist. As a matter of fact, even an hour ago does not exist, and, therefore, all the things that belonged to yesterday or to an hour ago are as dead as yesterday's newspaper; they are no part of our being unless we revive them in this moment.

Our demonstration is to maintain our integrity to the highest degree of which we are capable at any given moment. If we make a mistake, let us pick ourselves up and be sure that it does not happen again. It is only what we carry over into the present that hurts us—not what happened in the past, but what we carry over into the present of what happened in the past. If each of us could begin every day afresh with the realization, "I and my Father are one," it would make no difference what our mistakes were yesterday as long as they are not repeated today. It is only when we revive yesterday and bring it into today that it injures us. We do not live on yesterday's manna, but neither can we suffer from yesterday's lack of manna. It is only what we are and what we have this instant, what we are living in this instant, that counts. It is only we who, in memory, bring yesterday into today. We can bring yesterday into our deeds, also, by making the same mistakes today that we made yesterday.

If we, in this moment, revive our hates and fears and animosities of yesterday, they are alive and active in our experience today. Then we are subject to the punishment of cosmic law, because it is this moment in which we are in enmity or antagonism to the law of the Christ. But this moment let us bring ourselves to the realization:

Yesterday is gone forever; tomorrow will never come; there is only today; and today love is the fulfilling of the law. This moment I acknowledge the Christ as my being; I acknowledge the Christ as the life of my friend or enemy; I acknowledge the Christ alone.

Then, in this moment, we are Christ-consciousness. In this moment, we are aligned with cosmic law, and all the power of the Godhead is flowing through us to "forgive us our debts as we forgive our debtors, [to] lead us not into temptation," to hold us on the course leading to spiritual fulfillment. Let us hold steadfastly to this Christhood. "Go and sin no more." It makes no difference how scarlet our sins were a moment ago, if, in this moment, we realize the Christ—Christ as omnipotence, Christ as our individual being, Christ as the only power unto our experience. Then are we children of God, then are we aligned with the cosmic power, and all the forces of the world unite to uphold us, support us, sustain us, and maintain us.

"Neither do I condemn thee but go and sin no more." This is our moment of repentance. "Turn ye and live." This is our moment of adopting Christ; this is our moment of accepting Christ; this is the moment in which we acknowledge that no longer will we indulge in resentment, revenge, or retaliation, nor will we put on any armor with which to defend ourselves from somebody's evil deeds or thoughts, but in this moment we stand in our Christhood. We not only stand in our own Christhood, but we stand in the Christhood of every person. There is no such thing as standing in Christhood for ourselves unless we hold to the Christhood of every other person as well. When we see Christhood in this universe, when we see the Christ appearing in form as human, animal, or vegetable, then all the power of the cosmos works in us. It will work through even our body to raise it up, to resurrect it, to redeem it, to spiritualize it, so that even this body becomes the temple of the living God and not just a carnal or a mortal body. This carnal body is translated into its spiritual reality—but only in a moment of Christhood.

Yesterday—that is gone. Our old days—they are gone. Our animosities, jealousies, and bickerings—what about them? Under ordinary circumstances, they represent only human ignorance; but what happens when these are indulged in by those who have acknowledged the Christ? Then it becomes spiritual wickedness in high places. If a person has accepted the Christ—has put on the Robe and has adopted Christhood—and then goes back to the indulgence of these human errors, from him a double penalty is exacted because he understands the law and knowingly has violated it. He, then, is sinning consciously and not ignorantly. The only final word is, "Go and sin no more."

This life is not ours. This life is God's. We belong to God, and God is responsible for our life and for our fulfillment. Whatever of good takes place in our life is God in action; whatever of evil takes place is only in proportion as the word "I" is injected—I, John; I, Mary; I, Henry. Let there be no praise for us, no condemnation, and no weight of responsibility. When responsibility comes, let us be sure that we do not permit this human sense of "I" to come forth and say: "How can I accomplish this? How am I going to perform that? My strength is not sufficient; my bank account is not adequate." Jesus did not permit the word "I" to intrude when he was called upon to feed the five thousand. He acknowledged that he could do nothing of himself.

As we study, read, and meditate, we are developing a state of consciousness which recognizes the Father within as the only actor and the only activity, and we are paving the way for an actual God-experience. The moment we have a God-experience, we no longer live our own life: God lives

Its life as us. We have nothing to do but to be very peaceful and quiet. It is like looking over our shoulders, watching God unfold. We become beholders of God and God's activity, and then all sense of personal responsibility drops away. Early in the morning, we begin our day with a sense of expectancy of what the Father will present for us to do. Once the work is given us, a quiet smile comes in the remembrance that He that has given it to us, performs it. The entire day is filled with joy in watching the glory of the Father unfold as our individual experience.

We become beholders of God appearing as you and as me. And what about all the people out here in the world with whom we come in contact every day? They represent our finite concept of God, but actually all that is here is God manifested as the Son: the Father and the Son one; God, the Invisible, and the child, the visible. To see this is to be able to live as a beholder of God performing that which is given us to do, a beholder of God as the divine law of adjustment. When this is brought into family relationships, community relationships, capital and labor relationships, this law of adjustment operates to reveal the eternal harmony.

It is God's responsibility to see to it that we are grateful to one another, that we co-operate with one another, because these activities are love, and love is of God, not of man. Man is only the vehicle for its expression, the instrument for God's love to be expressed. We shall never glory in praise and we shall never be hurt by censure if the Christ is the motivating force in our life. Then that which is being praised is the Christ. If, however, that Christ is misunderstood, It may be condemned. There is no condemnation for the person who knows that the Christ, alone, is acting in him. With love and with grace, the Christ can dissolve whatever condemnation may come.

We are in bondage to the world and everyone in it as

long as we look to it for that which must come from God and can only come from God. Fear and worry as to whether or not we have sufficient understanding or wisdom to discharge our responsibilities are dispelled when we know that it is not our wisdom or our understanding, but God's wisdom, understanding, justice, and benevolence that govern all of us. The whole question revolves around the use and meaning of the words "I," "me," "mine"—my wisdom, my strength, or my understanding; your appreciation or your gratitude; and whether or not we have risen high enough to realize:

I am not concerned with whether anybody is grateful or anybody is loving or anybody is just. I renounce all that. I look for love, justice, recognition, reward, and compensation, in, of, and from God.

The moment we take that attitude we are free from the world.

The great Master said: "My doctrine is not mine, but his that sent me. If I speak of myself I bear witness to a lie." The whole teaching is that only God can perform, only God can love, only God can think, only God is the healing, feeding, and supplying agency, only God can express wisdom and joy. We can do all things through God, but without God we can do nothing; we are the vehicles through and as which God appears.

Eventually, we must give up the personal sense of selfhood with its heavy load of responsibility and let the divine Presence take over. We must begin with this minute. Everything that happens, happens now. This minute we can begin to realize:

Only God functions as my being; only God functions as any and every person on the face of the earth. I loose everyone in my experience; I let everyone go and look only to God for whatever it is that, heretofore, I was expecting from man.

That is the secret of life.

That is the secret of the first commandment. Only God is power: Never worship effect; worship only God. "Cease ye from man, whose breath is in his nostrils for wherein is he to be accounted cf. . . . Put not your faith in princes." It is the Father's good pleasure to give us the kingdom. Why, then, should we seek it from man? Why should we look to man for that which it is God's good pleasure to give us? Why do we look to parents, children, neighbors, or friends, when all the time *I* am come that we might be fulfilled.

The moment we live this life of the Spirit which is a sufficiency through Christ, none of the things that afflict the world will afflict us. In that moment, we bring ourselves into oneness with spiritual law. We look to the *I* of our own being to fulfill our every experience; we turn every responsibility over to the Christ of our being. As we live in that life, freeing everybody from the bondage of criticism, condemnation, and judgment, the whole world may collapse; but it will not collapse where we are, for it will not come nigh our dwelling. To the extent that we are willing to loose the world and let it go, are we free from the world, from the things of the world, and from the people of the world.

Loose man whose breath is in his nostrils, and he will never be a problem again. People resent, fight, and resist us, only in proportion as we have some hold on them. Only in proportion as we are looking to them for something, do they struggle to tear away from that bondage and have their freedom. The instant we give them their freedom and say: "You owe me nothing. My good is of God, so let us live together and share together," we free ourselves from all the hate, envy, and jealousy in the world. What is more important, we live in conscious union with God.

This is the secret of spiritual living. It is the secret of the mystical life. "I and my Father are one," and all that the Father has is mine. Does that have anything to do with anyone else in the world? When our reliance is on God, we can never be disappointed. God has never failed anyone. "I have never seen the righteous begging bread." The righteous are living in obedience to spiritual law, the law of having no other gods save only *Me*, loving their neighbor as themselves, praying for their enemies, forgiving seventy times seven, holding no one in bondage, but looking only to the Christ for their sufficiency in all things. The person who is living that life will never beg bread.

This constitutes righteousness: conscious union with God; the realization of God as Father, or as the creative principle; the realization of God as support and supply; the realization of God as the health of our countenance; the realization that our sufficiency is of God; the realization that only God can love, and therefore, we must not look to man for love, but let God's love flow through us to man and then claim no reward for it because it is of God and not of us.

The Way is secrecy and silence. Within us is a deep well of contentment, a vast, all-embracing silence into which we relax and through which all good appears to us. Seek the atmosphere of God's presence and rest; seek the consciousness of His presence. "In quietness and in confidence shall be our strength." He leadeth us beside the still waters and into green pastures that we may rest from strife, from struggle, and from effort, and behold the glory of God risen round about us. This is the inner meaning of The Infinite Way. In this understanding, we have entered that sanctuary where the noises of the world never reach, and where the troubles of the world never penetrate. Where is this? It is in the very depths of our own consciousness, in the very depths of our own Soul, when we have refrained from strife, from struggle, and from taking thought.

CHAPTER X

THE VISION TO BEHOLD

In the beginning in the Edenic days, man was complete, whole, and harmonious—one with God. By the grace of God everything flourished, and there was peace. What man is now striving to attain in his search for God is the re-establishment of that Edenic state of complete peace and harmony, a state in which we are not at war with one another, but in love with one another; a state in which we do not deprive others, but share and give to others.

The hope of man has been that by finding some supernatural power he would be able to recapture that state of bliss on earth. It must be clear to every thinking person, however, that in his attempt to find harmony, man has been searching in the wrong way and in the wrong place. Individual harmony and world peace will never be established by searching for some supernatural power. Man's need is to re-establish himself in his original Edenic estate which is oneness with God.

Hundreds of years of frustration and failure should have

THE VISION TO BEHOLD

proved to the world that it is not the work of a God to do this for us: It is our work to do it for ourselves by establishing that original relationship of oneness. The Master said, "Ye shall know the truth and the truth shall make you free." Nowhere does he indicate that this is God's responsibility. Time and time again he reiterates that it is our responsibility: "Ye shall know the truth . . . Ye shall love the Lord thy God . . . Ye shall love thy neighbor as thyself . . . Ye shall pray for the enemy . . . Ye shall forgive seventy times seven . . . Ye shall bring the tithes into the storehouse." In no place and at no time does he place the responsibility for our sense of separation from God upon God, but upon us. To us is addressed the entire teaching of Jesus Christ—not to God, to us.

Lest, however, we should flounder, the Master has given us the way, the where, the when, and the how of this demonstration of unity: The way is prayer; the where is the kingdom of God within us; the when is now—this moment of Christhood; the how is action. At first, the secrets that have been given to the God-inspired men and women of all time can only be taught by imparting that which is called the letter of truth. Through the letter of truth, we learn to stop that aimless searching for God, that fruitless praying to a far-off God for something, that senseless wishing and hoping that some form of worship will be sufficiently pleasing to God to influence Him in our behalf; and we come into a recognition, not only that there is a God, but that God is the inner Self of our own being, a God not separate and apart from us to be worshiped from afar off, but actually a God closer than breathing, nearer than hands and feet.

The correct letter of truth keeps us from indulging in idle daydreaming or in the false hope that some miracle is going to bring God or his messenger down on a cloud to wave a magic wand, and then all our troubles will disappear. On the contrary, this simple truth of the Master causes us to withdraw our gaze from upward and outward and turn it in the only direction in which we can find peace and harmony—within ourselves. When our attention has shifted from the outer to the inner, we can take the next step taught by every great master: Seek *Me* within; seek; knock; if necessary plead, but always within.

The vision of oneness must ever be a beacon light on our upward path: "I and my Father are one." Through inner contemplation of the Father within, ultimately, "I and my Father" mold and melt into one, and that ancient unity is established. Now, "I and my Father are one" is no longer an intellectual perception, but "I and my Father are one" becomes a demonstrable relationship, visible in its fruits. No longer do we seek for favors; no longer is there any need of favors; the Spirit within is unfolding, revealing, and disclosing Itself, acting in and through us. The world's acceptance of a power of good and a power of evil no longer enslaves us; we rest serenely at peace in one power. There are no powers to fight; there are no powers to fear! That is why we do not have to pray for some great power to do something. Those things which for centuries the world has considered power and for which it has been seeking a God, are not power. The power is in the still small voice.

At some period or other in this search for God, that indissoluble union with the Father begins to be recognized and felt. The letter of truth becomes less important and the Spirit becomes the vital thing. The Spirit which we have known only through the reading of books now comes alive in us, and we *live* truth. These truths, lived and practiced, become the very presence of God. God is revealed as the creative, maintaining, and sustaining principle—not our servant or our tool, nor something existing for the purpose of bestowing favors upon us, but the infinite wisdom of this universe, the divine love unto all that is. Now the Mes-

sianic message given to the world two thousand years ago is
beginning to be fulfilled in us: God is love. No God can
operate in our experience except through love, and we must
become the instrument through which that love is permitted to escape. Henceforth, the commandment "Thou
shalt love the Lord thy God with all thy heart and thy
neighbor as thyself" will have no significance to us except
in proportion as we are loving. This commandment has
been known for thousands of years. Today—now, in this
moment of Christhood—this teaching should be put into
action; there should be an end to the meaningless repeti-
tion of those words. Now that commandment must be
brought down into the heart and lived, implemented by obedience to the Master's injunction: "Do unto others as you
would have others do unto you. . . . Forgive seventy times
seven. . . . Do not condemn. . . . Do not judge."

There is no miracle-God except the miracle that becomes
evident in the living of our oneness with God. That is the
miracle. Knowing the truth with the mind does not guarantee that it will be put into action: It is when truth seeps
down from the mind and penetrates the heart that the
Spirit reigns, and love is enthroned. The letter of truth
serves as a reminder to bring us into the livingness of that
truth. There are times when, through a sense of separation
from God, truth seems to be so far away that we must sit
down and, by engaging in a discussion with ourselves, consciously remember that the Lord in the midst of us is mighty:

*What am I looking for? A god somewhere? No, God's in
His heaven, and all is well with the world. God is already
about His own business, and the Son of God is already
about the Father's business.*

*What am I seeking? A mythological God up in the sky?
A statue? A graven image? Am I looking for a man or a
woman to influence God in my behalf? No, I and the Father*

are one, and only in my oneness with God can I have the
peace that I desire; only in the fulfillment of that oneness,
of that love, which exists between God and the Son of God,
and between the Son of God and God; only in the realization
that my heavenly Father is closer to me than breathing,
and nearer than hands and feet, and that it is His good
pleasure to give me the kingdom—only in that, does a love
flow out, a love that seems to be flowing from me to God
and from God back to me, but which is actually an interac-
tion within the oneness of my being in the realization of
my oneness with the Father.

The Master taught that human beings of themselves can
do nothing, but human beings reunited with the Father
within them—no longer two but one—can do all things, and
they are the eternal and immortal Sons of God. When the
Spirit of God is upon us and dwells in us, then do we become the Sons of God. And who can do this for us but we
ourselves? The way has been given to us and that way is
prayer and meditation. It is an enlightened form of prayer
such as Elijah taught Elisha: Look up and see if you can
behold me rising on a cloud. Lift up your eyes unto the hills
from whence cometh your help. Behold the kingdom of
God within you.

Elisha sought to succeed to the mantle of Elijah; he
longed to be a great prophet—he wanted that robe of
Christliness. When Elijah was about to rise into a higher
state of consciousness, Elisha asked one great favor of him,
that "a double portion of thy spirit be upon me"—that
Elijah's mantle be given to him. But Elijah, one of the very
great, spiritually illumined souls of all time, knew that he
could not give his mantle to Elisha, but that Elisha could
earn it—could deserve it, be worthy of it, be ready for it—
and he told him how: "If thou see me when I am taken from
thee, it shall be so unto thee"—if when I rise out of sight,

if you behold me as I am, rising on a cloud out of sight, then my mantle shall fall upon your shoulders.

Elijah could not bestow his great spiritual wisdom even upon Elisha, but Elisha could achieve that spiritual consciousness for himself if his vision could rise so high that he could recognize that there is no death; there is no separation: There is only a rising in consciousness. If he himself could ascend to that supreme height of consciousness, then he would be a prophet of the stature of Elijah. In this he succeeded. Elisha was illumined to such an extent that he saw Elijah rising in a whirlwind into heaven, and by virtue of his conscious oneness with God, he saw the immortality of individual being and the eternality of man in its fullness and completeness.

The responsibility is upon us to behold the vision and then to put it into action. Teachers there have ever been and always will be; the illumined we have always had with us; but the Master said that the workers are few. The laborers are few who are willing to become reconciled to God, who are willing to contemplate the Soul within themselves and then let it flow out in deeds of love. "If a man say, I love God, and hateth his brother, he is a liar: for he that loveth not his brother whom he hath seen, how can he love God whom he hath not seen?" If the Master had not washed the feet of the disciples, the world never would have learned that the function of the Master was to be a servant. The function of the illumined is to serve those who do not yet know their true identity. Our function, as seekers after God and as truth students, is not to be a master over multitudes, but to be a servant unto multitudes—not to take from the multitudes, but to give unto the multitudes.

The kingdom of God is neither "Lo here! or, Lo there!" but within our own being. And how do we find that kingdom? By love: Love this Lord that is in the midst of you and demonstrate that love by your love for your neighbor, the neighbor who is not only your friend, but the neighbor who is your enemy and the neighbor who despitefully uses you and persecutes you. According to the Master, it is better to give time and attention to one lowly sinner than to the ninety and nine who are managing very well on their own. As long as there is any individual, be he saint or sinner, reaching out for help, it becomes our obligation and our duty to answer that call. Everyone is not ready to respond on the spiritual level for he may not be ready for the complete unfoldment of spiritual truth, but because he is our neighbor, we can at least help him on his level of consciousness while he is evolving to a higher state of consciousness. Let us, with patience, wait for the one or two to come to us—the twelve, the seventy, the two hundred—and then share this bread of life with them, share the wine and the water. These are the ones who will be able to appreciate its taste; they will enjoy it and, moreover, they will be able to assimilate it.

Let us hold that which we have as a pearl of great price and show it to the world by a living of it rather than by a talking about it. When someone comes, who is attracted not just by the loaves and fishes, but who perceives the nature of this truth, and asks for bread, wine, water, and life eternal, let us share it to the fullest extent of our ability. No one is ever going to be called upon to do something greater than his understanding because the only call is to sit peacefully and quietly until the Spirit of the Lord God is upon him, and then he can voice anything that comes to his lips, or voice nothing at all.

Love is the answer: the love of God, the love of truth, and the love of our neighbor. From this time forth, it should be the function and the mission of those of us who are practicing the Presence to reveal that God is experienced only in proportion as God is expressed. God is experienced in proportion as God is permitted to flow out from us in the form of love, truth, service, and dedication. The power of love must be released from within ourselves.

The presence of God is made available on earth as it is in heaven through the experience of conscious union. That calls for as great an effort and as much wisdom as Elisha demonstrated when he beheld his master rising in a whirlwind, or as limitless vision as the disciples had when they witnessed the Transfiguration. The Master was capable of transfiguration, but something was necessary on the part of the disciples for them to have the vision to behold it. The Master could not reveal transfiguration; he could only experience it: The revelation had to take place in the consciousness of those who were present in order for them to be able to witness it.

Many miracles may occur in our experience, but only those who are themselves sufficiently attuned to behold them will be conscious of what has happened. Do we have eyes and do not see? Do we have ears and do not hear? The miracle of Transfiguration is awaiting our beholding. It is taking place in this world every day, every minute of every day, and at the very place where we are standing, if we can but open our eyes to behold the vision of that which is. The Transfiguration is not an experience of two thousand years ago, nor is the Crucifixion, the Resurrection, or the Ascension. Those are experiences that are occurring every moment of every day, wherever there is an illumined soul to behold them.

This very place upon which we stand is holy ground, if we have the vision to behold Elijah rising, if we have the vision to behold the Master in the experience of Transfiguration, if we have the vision to behold the Resurrection and the Ascension. It is all up to us: It is up to you; it is up to me. To what degree do we want to see transfiguration? To what degree do we want to witness resurrection and ascension? To that degree will be the experience of it. The means of it? Prayer—the prayer of inner contemplation, the prayer of inner meditation, the prayer of expectancy which always knows that, at any moment, the Father is revealing Itself; in every moment, the Father is revealing Itself.

God cannot force Itself into anybody's mind or heart or soul. It is the individual who must open himself to God. The life of Gautama, the Buddha, illustrates this point. On the day when Gautama first realized that there was evil in the world—sin, disease, poverty, and death—he was horrified, tormented to such an extent that he left his princely position, his enormous wealth, and probably, what is more important to any man, his wife and child. He left all of that and wandered away as a beggar, seeking truth for the one purpose of discovering the great secret which would remove sin, disease, and limitation from the earth.

This was such a passionate call with him that he followed any teacher and any teaching which promised to lead him to the answer. For twenty-one years he roamed and wandered, sitting at the feet of first one teacher and then another, following the practices of one teaching after another, always with but one heart-hunger: What is the power that will remove these evils from off the earth? And when he had given up all hope that the teachings and the teachers would reveal this to him, having seated himself beneath the Bodhi tree, he meditated day and night until the great revelation was given to him: These evils are not real, they are illusion; people accept them and then hate, fear, love, or worship them, when actually they have no existence except in the mind of man. The mind of man has created the evil conditions of the world and the mind of man perpetuates them.

It was not God who forced Himself upon Gautama and made him the enlightened Buddha. It was Gautama's devotion to the search for God, his passion for it, which was evidenced by his sacrifice of himself and his willingness to travel the length and breadth of India, seeking wherever there might be some small facet of truth until, in that moment, when he rose to a sufficient degree of spiritual illumination, truth revealed itself to him.

We do not actually know what led Christ Jesus to the experience which ultimately established him in his full Christhood, but this we do know: When he came to reveal what he had learned, he said, "Ask, and it shall be given you; seek, and ye shall find; knock, and it shall be opened unto you," indicating that it is in the degree that we seek and knock and plead, in the degree that we make a way within ourselves that the answer will be given to us. It will not come by sitting and waiting aimlessly and superstitiously for some God to force Itself upon us.

If we wish to become a master of music, of languages, or of art, God can inspire us; but we must dig, search, study, and practice, until that which we are seeking opens up within our own being. I do believe that it is God who plants in us the desire to find Him, and that without God's performing that initial function, we never would succeed. There is a power of God in each one of us forcing us to "knock and seek," but there is no God that can do it for us: No God can save us the years of sitting alone and working alone, trying to penetrate the veil in order to rise to that higher state of consciousness where we, too, can behold the risen Jesus, the ascended Christ. Only God could make Gautama stay on that path for twenty-one years, but only Gautama could persist and fight and pray until the veil parted and the vision became clear.

So with us. No miracle-working, far-off God will come down to earth to change us and reveal Its wonders and Its glories while we sit idly by as spectators. The burden is upon you and upon me. The very fact that we can sit for hours at a time, quietly, and at peace with the message of God is proof that the Spirit of God has touched us and has invited us to the feast. The degree of knocking, searching,

seeking, and pleading, and the degree of intensity with
which we knock, search, seek, and plead will determine the
degree of the vision we behold. Some will see a little, and
some will see a great deal, and some will see it all—*in the
degree.*

Above all things, success will depend upon secrecy. Secrecy and sacredness go hand in hand. If the search for
God is sacred to us, we shall never permit it to be defiled
by exposing it to the profane. We will not wear a sacred
robe in public, nor put on a sanctimonious face before our
friends. Outwardly, we shall appear to be as all other men
and women, but inwardly, we shall remember the sacred
nature of the search for God and hold it a secret to be seen
only by its fruitage, but never by our voicing it, nor by
our trying to proselyte. That does not mean that we should
withhold the cup of cold water, but having offered our cup
of cold water, let us remember that those to whom it has
been offered will have to drink of it for themselves, and
they must be the ones to come back and ask for more.

Everyone is entitled to whatever measure or kind of religion he may want, or he is entitled to have none. That is
the freedom which we must give to each other—to let each
have his own will within himself until that seed is planted
that sends him out in search of the Holy Grail. If we hold
the Christ-child within ourselves and never expose it, the
fruitage of it will be so glorious that we shall be sought out,
a nation sought after, and people will want to eat of our
fruit, meat, and bread, and to drink of our water.

The object of the search—union, to be united again with
that from which we became separated after the expulsion
from the Garden of Eden, or after the experience of the
prodigal son. When the prodigal reaches that last mile,
that last depth of poverty, then it is that his footsteps turn
back to the Father's house, to be reunited with the Father.
That is not an experience in time or space; that is an experi-

ence which takes place within your consciousness and mine. When we have reached that last place beyond which there seems to be nothing but despair, even death—when we have reached that place, something within us turns us to the spiritual life, and then slowly we begin to travel the path back to our Father's house.

We, who are aspirants on the spiritual path, have reached the place where we know that the kingdom of God is to be found within ourselves: We have reached the place where we now know that all of the outer forms are useless in our search; we have reached the place where we know what we are seeking—reunion with That from which we seem to have become separated. That cannot take place outside our own being. No one can do this for us. Only in our inner meditation, in our inner contemplation, can we find it, when inwardly we have become gentle and when we feel a depth of love that would almost make us open our arms to take the whole world in, as Jesus would like to have done for Jerusalem: "Oh, how I would love to put my arms around you and draw you in, but ye would not. Come to me and feel the warmth of love." We, too, shall find that they would not, they will not—except the few.

We, who are practicing the Presence, are of the few who know what ultimately will save the world. It is above all things the acknowledgment that no man on earth is our father: There is one universal Father within us, and united with Him, we are united with every spiritual child of God throughout the world. Our love for God constitutes our love for the people of the world. We no longer hate; we no longer fear. We need not punish; we need not seek vengeance: We need only withdraw into ourselves and contemplate our oneness with God and with one another.

Our function is to love, to love all men with a love which stems from the realization that our union with God constitutes our integrity. In this love, there is no temptation to resort to devious means such as lying, cheating or chicanery in a futile effort to maintain ourselves because, in our union with God, we have access to the mind of God which is infinite intelligence and the source of all life, truth, and love. We are fed, not by our position or our accumulated wealth, but by the bread which is within our own being, by the wine, the water, and the meat.

This is the secret which heals disease, reforms sin, overcomes lack and limitation, and unites us, not only with our immediate circle, but with every individual on the face of the globe, even if those individuals have not yet become aware of us or of the love that we feel for them, and even if they have not yet become aware of the fact that we have drawn a circle and included them in that circle. They may not immediately know it but we know it, and our knowing it is sufficient because that knowledge transmits itself to those included within that circle.

We sit inside ourselves looking out upon the world without the use of force of any kind, even mental force, withdrawing all opposition; and this renunciation of the use of the world's weapons is the only means by which peace on earth will be established. It may take years; it may take centuries before He come whose right it is, that is, before this is demonstrated on earth as it is in heaven, because there are only a few people out of the billions on earth who are consciously practicing the Presence. That little leaven, however, must leaven the whole lump.

Do you not see that if what you are reading is true and you feel it, you will be inspired to live this truth? Then can you not also see that wherever you are in time or space, if you so love God that you will spend many periods a day, even brief ones, tabernacling in the temple of your own inner being with this Presence, one here and one there will be drawn to you? As an individual, you may believe that you can do nothing; you are only one in four billion. But if you look at the great spiritual lights of the past, you will understand how untrue that is, because you will see how one individual called Gautama, the Buddha; one individual called Jesus, the Christ; one individual like St. Paul influenced not only his own generation but the generations that followed him and will influence generations yet to come. Think of the widespread influence that just one individual can have through God's grace—one individual whose only purpose in life is to find God and to solve the mysteries of life.

This is the message I give you: I do not care how great you are or how mighty—of yourself, you are nothing. I do not care how small you are or how insignificant—you are nothing, until the grace of God touches you, until the Spirit of God dwells in you, until the finger of the Christ has moved you. From then on, you are infinite—infinite in expression, infinite and eternal in life, infinite in power, infinite in experience, infinite as an example and as a wayshower. But never is it you, never is it I: It is the Spirit of God which can find outlet only as human consciousness, as your consciousness and mine. All the truth of the world remains hidden except in proportion as it can find a human consciousness through which or as which it can flow out to the world of men.

Whatever or wherever your community is, this truth may remain locked up in space unless someone in that community is the instrument which gives it outlet there. God does not act without a consciousness through which to act: God must have saints, sages, and seers. Let us put it this way: God must have lowly carpenters; God must have mighty princes; God must have simple housewives: Of these, God makes saints or sages to send out into the world to carry the light. Almost all those who have attained any degree of spiritual stature in the world have been the little nobodies of the world, and only the inspired light which they experienced made them more than that to the world.

In and of themselves, they were nothing; in and of yourself, you are nothing; but in your conscious union with God, all that God is, you are. All that the Father hath is yours. The very place whereon you stand becomes holy ground because "I and my Father" are there.

You can rise no higher in consciousness than to that place where the spiritual Presence enters the heart, and you realize it has happened—the Presence is within you. A new dimension has entered your heart when you entertain the Presence, but I must say to you that it is your responsibility to nurture it. That is the only way to be sure that you will not lose what you have gained. What you have gained is only a Babe; you must let it develop into full Christhood: Many times a day turn your thought as if in the direction of your heart—not because your physical heart has anything to do with your spiritual demonstration, but because the heart is symbolic of love. Thinking of the heart as a symbol of love, as a symbol of the resting place of the Christ within you, turn your thought several times each day to that heart in recognition that the Babe is enthroned there, that the Christ has entered, and that It lives with you. It is you who must keep the Babe from wandering out of your heart and getting lost. It is there, but I say to you that it is a Babe: You must watch It; you must nurse It; you must acknowledge It, love It. Watch It grow as you learn the ways of loving God and of loving man. No improvement has ever been discovered, no alteration has ever been made in the two great commandments, "Thou shalt love the Lord thy God with all thy heart, and with all thy soul, and with all thy mind . . . and . . . Thou shalt love thy neighbor as thyself."

No longer plead with God for things; let this Babe do all that for you. It will not have to plead: It will experience Itself as the added things. Do not look to God for favors and do not look to God for strange powers to do things for you. Turn your gaze now to the place where you have already felt that gentle Presence. Smile at It. Secretly and sacredly know that It is there and that It is fulfilling Its function and is about the Father's business. This Babe is given unto you to restore the lost years of the locusts and to return you to the Father's house and to your conscious union with God.

It is the function of this Babe to reveal that you are living in the midst of Eden where you will always be tempted with only one temptation: There is only one evil in the Garden of Eden, only one sin—the belief in the power of good and evil. You, sitting back inside your own temple, must be able to look at that tree of the knowledge of good and evil at all times and resist the temptation to believe in it. You, yourself, must be able to say:

Beautiful as you look, or horrible as you look, I now know there is no truth in you. There is no power for good or for evil in any form, that is, in any person, place, thing, circumstance, or condition. God in the midst of me is the only good, the only power, and the only presence. The only evil there is, is the belief in a selfhood or a condition separate and apart from God.

Even when you have overcome for yourself every form in which this one temptation may appear, the problems of the world will tempt you: storms at sea, disaster, war, poverty, and disease; but whatever the temptation, it will always be the one great temptation—to accept two powers. This is when you must turn to the Christ within:

The Christ within me is my assurance that only It has power—the Son of God, the Spirit of God in me. It will never leave me nor forsake me as long as I realize and recognize It and as long as I live the life It tells me to live. I took to It for guidance; I look to It for wisdom. Whenever a question is presented to my mind, I look down toward my heart, and the answer comes forth in whatever form is necessary.

Oh, do not be too literal about this. Sometimes this Presence will seem to be looking at you from over your shoulder or sitting right on your shoulder; sometimes It will appear as a face in front of you, sometimes smiling, but always reassuring. Keep It alive.

The presence of this Christ, gentle and small as It may be, is the substance of every experience that you will have on the outer plane. Seek neither health, nor wealth, nor fame, nor fortune. Seek first the realization of this inner kingdom and be a beholder as these outer things are added unto your experience. Do not hesitate to turn to It for revelation. Why should not revelation be given to you as well as to others who have lived before you? "God is no respecter of persons." Gautama was only the Buddha because he worked for twenty-one years to receive illumination; Jesus was only the Christ because he gave himself to the world; and you will be whatever degree of love there is in you for God and for your neighbor. You will be whatever you permit yourself to be, but only by acknowledging that you, yourself, can never be anything; it is this gentle Presence that you have felt that is to carry you throughout your days back into conscious union with God.

You know what the goal of life is—to be reunited with the Father, to be consciously one with God. You know the way—the prayer of inner contemplation and meditation, the recognition of the Christ, the love of God, and the love of man. Now carry this message in your mind where you will always remember the principles; and in your heart, dwell upon the gift which has been given you, delivered to you from the Father—the gift of the realized Presence within you. Bless It always that It may increase.